must**sees**

CHARLESTON
SAVANNAH AND THE
SOUTH CAROLINA COAST

Edmondston-Alston House/©Janette Siler/Michelin

MICHELIN

mustsees **Charleston, Savannah and the South Carolina Coast**

Editorial Director	Cynthia Clayton Ochterbeck
Editor	Gwen Cannon
Principal Writer	M. Linda Lee
Contributing Writers	Gwen Cannon, Claiborne Linvill
Production Manager	Natasha G. George
Cartography	Peter Wrenn
Photo Research	Nicole D. Jordan
Proofreader	M. Linda Lee
Layout	Nicole D. Jordan, Natasha G. George
Cover & Interior Design	Chris Bell
Cover Design & Layout	Natasha G. George
Contact Us	Michelin Travel and Lifestyle North America
	One Parkway South
	Greenville, SC 29615, USA
	travel.lifestyle@us.michelin.com
	www.michelintravel.com
	Michelin Travel Partner
	Hannay House
	39 Clarendon Road
	Watford, Herts WD17 1JA, UK
	www.ViaMichelin.com
	travelpubsales@uk.michelin.com
Special Sales	For information regarding bulk sales, customized editions and premium sales, please contact us at:
	travel.lifestyle@us.michelin.com
	www.michelintravel.com

Michelin Travel Partner

Société par actions simplifiées au capital de 11 629 590 EUR
27 cours de l'Ile Seguin - 92100 Boulogne Billancourt (France)
R.C.S. Nanterre 433 677 721

© 2013 Michelin Travel Partner
ISBN 978-2-06717984-4
Printed: July 2012
Printed and bound in Italy

Note to the reader:
While every effort is made to ensure that all information printed in this guide is correct
and up-to-date, Michelin Travel Partner accepts no liability for any direct, indirect or
consequential losses howsoever caused so far as such can be excluded by law. Admission
prices listed for sights in this guide are for a single adult, unless otherwise specified.

Welcome to Charleston, Savannah and the South Carolina Coast

Carriage ride in Savannah

Introduction

Introduction: Southern Charm

Must See

p 38

p 62

p 135

p 154

p 146

TABLE OF CONTENTS

★★★ ATTRACTIONS

Unmissable sights in and around Charleston, Savannah and the South Carolina Coast

For more than 75 years people have used the Michelin stars to take the guesswork out of travel. Our star-rating system helps you make the best decision about where to go, what to do, and what to see.

★★★	Absolutely Must See
★★	Really Must See
★	Must See
No Star	See

Sights below are located in South Carolina unless otherwise specified.

 # ACTIVITIES

**Unmissable activities in
Charleston, Savannah and the
South Carolina Coast**
**We recommend every activity in
this guide, but the Michelin Man
highlights our top picks.**

Beaches
Folly Beach County Park *p 63*
Huntington Beach
  State Park *p 121*
Jekyll Island beaches *p 155*

Festivals
Charleston Wine +
  Food Festival *p 84*
St. Patricks Day (Savannah) *p 146*

For Kids
James Island County Park *p 96*
Alligator Adventure *p 126*
Myrtle Waves Water Park *p 126*

Hotels and Spas
The Sanctuary and Spa *p 116, 176*
The Cloister and Spa *p 116, 185*
Afternoon Tea at Charleston
  Place Hotel *p 176*
Planters Inn *p 178*
Two Meeting Street Inn *p 180*
Jekyll Island Club Hotel *p 186*

Nightlife
Pavilion Bar for
  a rooftop cocktail *p 78*
Blind Tiger Pub *p 110*
High Cotton Maverick Bar
  & Grill *p 111*

Restaurants
Hank's Seafood Restaurant *p 164*
Husk *p 160*
Island Café & Deli *p 170*
Elizabeth on 37th *p 173*
The Crab Shack *p 175*

Theater and the Arts
Footlight Players *p 102*
Sottile Theatre *p 103*
The Have Nots!
  comedy improv *p 112*

Tours
Carriage Tours of the
  Historic District *p 78*
Ghosts of Charleston Tour *p 80*
Harbor Cruise Tours *p 80*
Savor the Flavors of
  Charleston Tour *p 82*

STAR ATTRACTIONS

CALENDAR OF EVENTS

Listed below is a selection of the most popular annual events for Charleston, the Carolina Coast, and Georgia, Savannah and the Golden Isles. Please note that dates may vary year to year.

For more detailed information, contact the convention and visitors bureaus listed on p 10 and p 18.

January

Lowcountry Oyster Festival
843-577-4030
Boone Hall Plantation,
Mt. Pleasant, SC
www.charlestonrestaurant
association.com

February

Black Heritage Festival
912-358 4309
Various locations, Savannah, GA
www.savannahblackheritage
festival.com
Gullah Celebration
843-255-7304
Hilton Head Island, SC
www.gullahcelebration.com

March

Canadian American Days
Festival (CanAm Days)
843-626-7444
Myrtle Beach, SC
www.grandstrandevents.com
Charleston Wine+ Food Festival
843-727-9998
Downtown, Charleston, SC
www.charlestonwineand
food.com
Festival of Houses and Gardens
843-722-3405
Historic District, Charleston, SC
www.historiccharleston.org/
news_events/festival.htlm
St. Patrick's Day Celebration
912-944-0455
Various locations, Savannah, GA
http://.savannahvisit.com

April

Cooper River Bridge Run
843-856-1949
Charleston, SC
www.bridgerun.com
Family Circle Cup Tennis
Tournament
800-677-2293
Family Circle Tennis Center
Charleston, SC
www.familycirclecup.com
Grand Strand Fishing Rodeo
843-916-7276
Myrtle Beach, SC (Apr 1–Oct 31)
www.GrandStrandFishing
Rodeo.com
Legends of Golf, PGA
Champions Tour
912-236-1333
Westin Savannah Harbor Golf
Resort & Spa, Savannah, GA
www.pgatour.com
SCDA Sidewalk Arts Festival
912-525-5000
Forsyth Park, Savannah, GA
www.scad.edu

May

Annual Sun Fun Festival
843-626-7444
Myrtle Beach, SC
www.grandstrandevents.com
Piccolo Spoleto (May-June)
843-724-7305
Various locations, Charleston, SC
www.piccolospoleto.org
Spoleto (May-June)
843-579-3100
Various locations, Charleston, SC
www.spoletousa.org

July

Beaufort Water Festival
843-524-0600
Waterfront Park, Beaufort, SC
www.bftwaterfestival.com

Fourth of July on the River
912-234-0295
River St., Savannah, GA
www.riverstreetsavannah.com

Patriots Point 4th of July Blast
866-831-1720
Patriots Point, Mt. Pleasant, SC
www.patriotspoint.org

August

**Barbecue Championship &
Bluegrass Festival**
843-884-4371
Boone Hall Plantation,
Mt. Pleasant, SC
www.boonehallplantation.com

September

MOJA Arts Festival
843-724-7305
Various locations, Charleston, SC
www.mojafestival.com

Savannah Jazz Festival
912-920-1317
Forsyth Park, Savannah, GA
www.savannahjazzfestival.org

Taste of Charleston
843-577-4030
Boone Hall Plantation,
Mt. Pleasant, SC
www.charlestonrestaurant
association.com

Taste of Savannah
912-232-1223
International Trade & Convention
Center, Savannah, GA
www.tourismleadership
council.com

**Fall Tour of Homes &
Gardens (Sept-Oct)**
843-722-4630
Historic District, Charleston, SC
www.preservationsociety.org

October

Beaufort Shrimp Festival
843-525-6644
Waterfront Park, Beaufort, SC
www.downtownbeaufort.com

Latin American Festival
843-795-4386
North Charleston Wannamaker
County Park, Charleston, SC
www.ccprc.com

Oktoberfest
912-234-0295
River St., Savannah, GA
http://riverstreetsavannah.com

Pirate Fest
912-786-5393
Tybee Island, GA,
www.tybeepiratefest.com

**Plantation Days at Middleton
Place (Oct-Nov)**
800-782-3608
Middleton Place, Charleston
www.middletonplace.org

November

Penn Center Heritage Days
843-838-2432
Penn Center, St. Helena Island, SC
www.penncenter.com

**Holiday Festival of Lights
(Nov-Dec)**
843-795-4386
James Island County Park
James Island, SC
www.ccprc.com

December

Holiday Parade of Boats
843-724-7414
Charleston Harbor
www.charlestonarts.org

Holiday Tour of Homes
912-308-6755
Historic District, Savannah, GA
www.dnaholidaytour.com

CALENDAR OF EVENTS

PRACTICAL INFORMATION

Seasonal Temperatures in Charleston				
	Jan	**Apr**	**Jul**	**Oct**
Avg. High	58°F / 14°C	74°F / 23°C	89°F / 32°C	76°F / 24°C
Avg. Low	40°F / 4°C	57°F / 14°C	73°F / 23°C	60°F /16°C

WHEN TO GO

With its subtropical climate, the South Carolina Coast is a great place to visit year-round. The best times to come, weather-wise—spring and fall—are also the most crowded. Spring is a lovely time of year in Charleston; the popular Festival of Houses and Gardens *(see p 8)* is held in spring, as well as the famous Spoleto festival *(see Performing Arts)*. Summers in the Lowcountry are hot and humid—sometimes oppressively so—but that doesn't stop sun-seekers from packing the beaches up and down the coast. In fall, the beach crowds go home and golfers turn out in droves to enjoy the crisp, clear weather on area courses. Winters are usually mild—it's not uncommon to have 60-degree days in January. Hotel rates in Charleston plummet this time of year.

KNOW BEFORE YOU GO

Before you go, contact the following organizations to obtain maps and information about sightseeing, accommodations, travel packages and seasonal events. All visitor centers below are closed Jan 1, Thanksgiving Day & Dec 25:

Visitor Centers

Charleston Area Convention and Visitors Bureau
423 King St., Charleston, SC 29403
843-853-8000 or 800-774-0006;
www.charlestoncvb.com

Charleston Visitor Center
375 Meeting St.
800-774-0006;
www.charlestoncvb.com
Open year-round daily 8:30am–5pm.

Kiawah Island Visitor Center
22 Beachwalker Dr., Kiawah Island
800-774-0006;
www.charlestoncvb.com
Open year-round Mon–Fri 9am–3pm. Closed city holidays.

Mt. Pleasant Visitor Center
99 Harry M. Hallman Jr., Blvd.,
Mt. Pleasant
800-774-0006;
www.charlestoncvb.com.
Open year-round daily 9am–5pm.

Websites

Here are some additional websites to help you plan your trip:

www.charlestonlowcountry.com
www.accesscharleston.com
www.charleston.net

www.discovercharleston.com
www.charleston.com
www.discoversouthcarolina.com

In The News

Charleston's main daily newspaper is the *Post and Courier (www.charleston.net)*; the arts and entertainment supplement *Charleston Scene* is published every Thursday. Other periodicals include: *The Chronicle*, an African-American weekly; the *Charleston City Paper,* published weekly (www.charlestoncitypaper.com); *Skirt,* a free monthly magazine for women *(www.skirt.com)*; and *Charleston Magazine (www.charlestonmag.com)*, a monthly publication.

North Charleston Visitor Center

4975-B Centre Pointe Dr., North Charleston; 800-774-0006; www.charlestoncvb.com
Open year-round Mon–Sat 10am–5pm, Sun 1pm–4pm.

Santee Welcome Center

Mile Marker 99 on I-95, Santee; 800-774-0006; www.charlestoncvb.com
Open year-round daily 9am–5pm. Closed Dec 24.

International Visitors

Visitors from outside the US can obtain information from the Charleston Convention and Visitors Bureau *(www.charlestoncvb.org)* or from the US embassy or consulate in their country of residence. For a complete list of American consulates and embassies abroad, visit the US State Department Bureau of Consular Affairs listing on the Internet at *www.usembassy.gov.*

Entry Requirements – Travelers entering the US under the Visa Waiver Program (VWP) must have a machine-readable passport valid 6 months beyond their expected stay. Any traveler without a machine-readable passport will be required to obtain a visa before entering the US. Citizens of VWP countries are permitted to enter the US for general business or tourist purposes for a maximum of 90 days without needing a visa. Requirements for the Visa Waiver Program can be found at the Department of State's Visa Services website *(http://travel.state.gov)*. All citizens of non-participating countries must have a visitor's visa. Upon entry, nonresident international visitors must present a valid passport and a round-trip transportation ticket. Canadian citizens must present a passport, Enhanced Driver's License or a Trust Traveler Program card (like NEXUS or FAST/Express).

US Customs – All articles brought into the US must be declared at the time of entry. Prohibited items include plant material; firearms (if not for sporting purposes); meat and poultry products. For information, contact the US Customs Service, 1300 Pennsylvania Ave. NW, Washington, DC 20229 *(703-526-4200; www.cbp.gov)*.

Driving in the US – Visitors bearing valid driver's licenses issued by

Exploring the Sights

The National Park Service and the City of Charleston host a website highlighting the numerous religious and community buildings of Charleston. Visit www.nps.gov/nr/travel/charleston for an overview of the many historic buildings that make up the Holy City, plus a map and full list of sights.

PRACTICAL INFORMATION

their country of residence are not required to obtain an International Driver's License. Drivers must carry vehicle registration and/or rental contract, and proof of automobile insurance at all times. Gasoline is sold by the gallon (1 gal=3.78 liters). Vehicles in the US are driven on the right-hand side of the road.

Time Zone – Charleston is located in the Eastern Time Zone (the same time zone as New York City), five hours behind Greenwich Mean Time.

GETTING THERE

By Air – Most major airlines service **Charleston International Airport (CHS)**, located 12 miles west of downtown off I-526 *(5500 International Blvd., 843-767-7010; www.chs-airport.com).*

A taxi from the airport to downtown costs approximately $25–$29. A more economical alternative, shuttles are available through Airport Ground Transportation, located outside baggage claim. Shuttle service to downtown is $12 per person.

By Train – Amtrak provides service to North Charleston *(8mi N of downtown)*; the rail station is located at 4565 Gaynor Avenue in North Charleston *(843-744-8264)*. For rates, schedules and reservations, contact Amtrak: 800-872-7245 or www.amtrak.com.

By Bus – For departures or arrivals by bus, the Greyhound Terminal is located in North Charleston *(3610 Dorchester Rd.; 843-744-4247)*. For rates, schedules and reservations, contact Greyhound: 800-231-2222 or 843-744-4247; www.greyhound.com.

By Car – Charleston lies about 52 miles southeast of I-95, the main north-south corridor on the East Coast. From I-95, or approaching from farther west, take I-26 directly to the city.

GETTING AROUND

By Car – Charleston is not laid out in a neat grid, but at 5.2 square miles, the peninsula on which the Historic District is located isn't difficult to navigate. Meeting Street and East Bay Street are the main

MUST KNOW

Important Numbers	
Emergency (Police/Ambulance/Fire Department, 24hrs)	911
Police (non-emergency, Mon–Fri 9am–6pm)	843-554-5700
Poison Control	800-222-1222
Medical Referral:	
Bon Secours-St. Francis/Roper Hospital	843-402-2273
	800-863-2273
Charleston County Medical Society	843-577-3613
East Cooper Regional Medical Center	843-881-0100
Medical University of South Carolina (MUSC)	843-792-2300
Trident Healthfinders	843-797-3463
Dental Emergencies: MUSC College of Dental Medicine	843-792-2101
24-hour Pharmacy: Walgreens, 907 Folly Rd.	843-795-2294

access points from the interstate highways. King Street, which is one-way going toward the Battery on the other side of Calhoun Street, is one of the main commercial thoroughfares. As you're driving, be cautious around the ever-present horse-drawn carriages that take visitors through the historic downtown. Use of a seat belt is required in South Carolina, and child safety seats are mandatory for children under 6 years and 80 pounds.

Parking – Metered street parking is available in Charleston, but it can be scarce, especially in high season and during business hours. Parking garages are a better (but pricey) option; you'll find them located at Aquarium Wharf and throughout the downtown area.

By Foot – Walking is the best way to get around the Historic District. Meandering down the streets is a great way to take in the stunning architecture and peek into the hidden private gardens. Although the area is generally very safe and heavily touristed, as in any city, you should beware of your surroundings when walking at night.

By Public Transportation – **Charleston Area Regional Transit Authority (CARTA)** runs an extensive network of public buses and trolleys linking downtown with West Ashley and North Charleston (843-724-7420; www.ridecarta.com). Bus stops are marked with signs.

Cooper River Bridge

Opened to traffic in 1929, the original 2.71-mile truss bridge over the Cooper River connected the city of Charleston to Mt. Pleasant. Another span was added next to the aging bridge in 1966. Today both the old bridges are gone—and an awesome new span has been constructed to replace them. Opened in July 2005, the Arthur Ravenel Jr. Bridge hovers 570 feet above the river and provides eight lanes for traffic, plus a pedestrian/bicycle lane. The signature diamond-tower design of one of North America's longest cable-stay bridges incorporates state-of-the-art seismic technology. For details, see www.cooperriverbridge.org.

PRACTICAL INFORMATION

Fare is $1.75 for a one-way trip *(exact change required; transfers cost 30¢)*. Children under age 6 ride free with a paying passenger. Purchase bus passes online (www.ridecarta.com) or from CARTA bus drivers *(daily passes only)*, at the Visitor Center *(375 Meeting St.)*, at area Piggly Wiggly grocery stores, and at the CARTA office *(36 John St)*.

- ◆ All-day pass – $6
- ◆ 3-day pass – $12
- ◆ 10-ride pass – $14
- ◆ 40-ride pass –$49

DASH Trolleys – Antique-looking green DASH trolleys operate three routes in Charleston's Historic Peninsula from Carta bus stops *(free of charge; for schedules 843-724-7420 or online at www.ridecarta.com)*.

By Taxi – The major cab companies in town are: Yellow Cab *(843-577-6565; $5 on the peninsula, then $1.75/mile)*; Charleston Green Taxi *(843-819-0846; $7-$15 downtown)*; and Charleston Black Cab Company *(843-216-2627)*.

ACCESSIBILITY

Disabled Travelers – Federal law requires that businesses (including hotels and restaurants) provide access for the disabled, devices for the hearing impaired, and designated parking spaces.

For further information, contact the Society for Accessible Travel and Hospitality (SATH), 347 Fifth Ave., Suite 605, New York, NY 10016 *(212-447-7284; www.sath.org)*.

All national parks have facilities for the disabled, and offer free or discounted passes. For details, contact the National Park Service *(Office of Public Inquiries, 1849 C St. NW, Room 1013, Washington, DC 20240; 202-208-4747; ww.nps.gov)*. Passengers who will need assistance with train or bus travel should give advance notice to Amtrak *(800-872-7245 or 800-523-6590/TDD; www.amtrak.com)* or Greyhound *(800-752-4841 or 800-345-3109/TDD; www.greyhound.com)*.

Reservations for hand-controlled rental cars should be made in advance with the rental company.

Local Lowdown – The following organizations provide detailed information about access for the disabled in Charleston:

- ◆ Access online **Charleston Area Convention and Visitors Bureau** *(www.charlestoncvb.com/visitors/travel_support/*

Property	Phone	Website
	Major hotel and motel chains with locations on the South Carolina Coast include:	
Best Western	800-780-7234	www.bestwestern.com
Comfort & Clarion Inns	877-424-6423	www.choicehotels.com
Days Inn	800-329-7466	www.daysinn.com
Hampton Inn	800-426-7866	www.hamptoninn.com
Hilton	800-774-1500	www.hilton.com
Holiday Inn	800-465-4329	www.holiday-inn.com
Sheraton/Starwood	800-325-3535	www.sheraton.com
Radisson	800-967-9033	www.radisson.com
Ramada	800-854-9517	www.ramada.com
Westin/Starwood	800-937-8461	www.westin.com

accessibility.html) for information regarding accessibility. The bureau will mail a printed copy to you if you are unable to access the guide online.

♦ Contact the **Charleston Area Regional Transit Authority (CARTA)** for information about disabled access to public transportation *(843-724-7420; www.ridecarta.com)*.

♦ **S.C. Dept. of Disabilities and Special Needs:** 888-376-4636.

Senior Citizens – Many hotels, attractions and restaurants offer discounts to visitors age 62 or older (proof of age may be required). AARP (formerly the American Association of Retired Persons) offers discounts to its members *(601 E St. NW, Washington, DC 20049; 888-687-2277; www.aarp.org)*.

ACCOMMODATIONS

For a list of suggested accommodations, *see Must Stay.*

Hotel Reservation Services
Historic Charleston Bed & Breakfast – *843-722-6606 or 800-743-3583. www.historic charlestonbedandbreakfast.com.* Regarding lodging in private homes in historic Charleston, this organization represents more than 50 bed-and-breakfast inns.

Lowcountry Reservation Service – Located at the Visitor Center *(375 Meeting St.),* this service offers in-person, same-day reservations for area hotels—often at a discount. No phone calls, please.

Hostels
A no-frills, inexpensive alternative to hotels, hostels appeal to budget travelers and students.

PRACTICAL INFORMATION

Accommodations at a Discount

Looking for a bargain? Try coming to Charleston mid-week in the summer. If you don't mind the sweltering heat and humidity, you can often find great room rates at some of the city's upscale hotels. If you're a golfer, be sure to ask about golf packages when you make your hotel reservations. Many accommodations along the coast will offer good rates that include a round or two at your choice of links.

NotSo Hostel – *156 Spring St. and 33 Cannon St. 843-722-8383. www.notsohostel.com. $24/night (dorms) $60-$70/night private rooms).* In a residential area downtown, Sprint Street hostel comprises three mid-19C houses with air-conditioned rooms, shared baths and kitchen. Cannon Street hostel is five blocks away. Breakfast and off-street parking are included in the rate.

AREA CODES

To call between different area codes, dial 1 + area code + seven-digit number. It's not necessary to use the area code to make a local call. Charleston, Kiawah, Isle of Palms, Myrtle Beach and Hilton Head: 843. Savannah and the Golden Isles of Georgia: 912

ELECTRICITY

Voltage in the US is 120 volts AC, 60 Hz. Foreign-made appliances may need AC adapters (available at specialty travel and electronics stores) and North American flat-blade plugs.

MONEY AND CURRENCY EXCHANGE

Visitors can exchange currency downtown at **American Express Travel Service** at **Abbot & Hill Travel** *(10 Carriage Lane; 843-556-9051).* For cash transfers, **Western Union** *(888-539-1108; www.western union.com)* has agents throughout the Charleston area.

Banks, stores, restaurants and hotels accept travelers' checks with photo identification.

To report a lost or stolen credit card: **American Express** *(800-528-4800);* **Diners Club** *(800-234-6377);* **MasterCard** *(800-307-7309);* **Visa** *(800-336-8472).*

TAXES AND TIPPING

Prices displayed in the US do not include the Charleston sales tax of 7%, which is not reimbursable (1% sales-tax discount is given to citizens age 85 and older), the 2% hospitality tax, or the hotel tax of 12%. It is customary to give a small gift of money—a tip—for services rendered, to waiters (15–20% of bill), porters ($1 per bag), hotel

Measurement Equivalents									
Degrees Fahrenheit	95°	86°	77°	68°	59°	50°	41°	32°	23°	14°
Degrees Celsius	35°	30°	25°	20°	15°	10°	5°	0°	-5°	-10°
1 inch = 2.5 centimeters		1 foot = 30.48 centimeters							
1 mile = 1.6 kilometers		1 pound = 0.45 kilograms							
1 quart = 0.9 liters		1 gallon = 3.78 liters							

Spectator Sports

Sport/Team	Venue	Phone/Website
Class-A Baseball Charleston RiverDogs	Joseph P. Riley Jr. Park	843-723-7241(info) 843-577-3647 (tickets) www.riverdogs.com
AA League/ECHL Hockey South Carolina Stingrays	North Charleston Coliseum	843-744-2248 (info) 843-743-3000 (tickets) www.stingrayshockey.com
A-League Soccer Charleston Battery	Blackbaud Stadium, Daniel Island	843-971-4625 (info) www.charlestonbattery.com

housekeeping staff ($1 per day) and cab drivers (15% of fare).

SPECTATOR SPORTS

Charleston has some minor-league sports teams, and offers a year-round calendar of sporting events. For more information about area sports, check out the website for the **Charleston Metro Sports Council**: *www.sportscouncil.org.*

SAVANNAH AND THE GOLDEN ISLES OF GEORGIA

Visitor Information

Before you go, contact these organizations for maps and information about sightseeing, accommodations, travel packages, recreational opportunities and seasonal events.

Savannah Convention and Visitors Bureau
101 E. Bay St., in the Historic District; 912-644-6400 or 877-728-2662; www.savannahvisit.com

Visitor Information Center
301 Martin Luther King Jr. Blvd. 912-944-0455; http://savannah visit.com

Golden Isles Convention and Visitors Bureau
4 Glynn Ave., Brunswick, GA 31520. 912-265-0620 or 800-933-2627; www.goldenisles.com

Getting There
By Air – **Savannah/Hilton Head International Airport (SAV)**, located 10 miles north of downtown, off I-95 *(400 Airways Ave.; 912-964-0514; www.savannahairport.com).* Two major airports provide service to Georgia's Golden Isles: **Savannah/Hilton Head International Airport** *(85mi north of Sea Island via I-95)* and **Jacksonville International Airport (JAX)**, located 70 miles south of Sea Island off I-95 *(2400 Yankee Clipper Dr., Jacksonville, FL; 904-741-4902; www.jia.aero).* **Brunswick Golden Isles Airport** *(500 Connole St., Brunswick, GA; 912-265-2070; www.glynncountyairports.com)* is served by Delta Connection.
By Car – From the north or south, reach Savannah and the Golden Isles via I-95, the main north-south corridor along the East Coast. From the west, get to Savannah via I-16, which intersects with I-75 in Macon, Georgia. If you're headed to the

PRACTICAL INFORMATION

17

Historic Downtown, stay on I-16; it takes you straight into town.

MYRTLE BEACH

Visitor Information
Stop for information and maps at one of these visitor centers:

Airport Welcome Center
1100 Jetport Rd.; 843-626-7444; www.myrtlebeachinfo.com
Open daily 8am–7pm.

Myrtle Beach Area CVB and Myrtle Beach Welcome Center
1200 N. Oak St.; 843-626-7444; www.myrtlebeachinfo.com
Open May–Labor Day Mon–Fri 8:30am–5pm, Sat 9am–5pm, Sun 10am–2pm. Rest of year Mon–Fri 8:30am–5pm, Sat 10am–2pm.

South Strand Welcome Center
3401 US 17 Bus. S., Murrells Inlet; 843-651-1010; www.myrtlebeachinfo.com
Open Apr–Labor Day Mon–Fri 8:30am–5pm, Sat 10am–5pm, Sun noon–5pm. Rest of year Mon–Fri 8:30am–5pm, Sat 10am–1pm.

When to Go
Unlike in Charleston, high season in Myrtle Beach is summer—despite searing heat. In off-season (late fall and winter), the weather is often mild, and you can get deep discounts on beachfront hotels.

Getting There
By Air – Myrtle Beach International Airport (MYR) is located south of 17th Avenue off Highway 15 *(1100 Jetport Rd.; 843-448-1589; www.flymyrtlebeach.com)*, and is served by Allegiant, Delta, Spirit, US Airways, United, Myrtle Beach Aviation and Porter. Major rental-car companies have facilities at the airport.
By Car – Myrtle Beach lies roughly halfway between New York City and Miami, Florida and an hour's drive from I-95, I-20, I-26 and I-40.

Getting Around
Driving in Myrtle Beach – The Grand Strand's commercial strip, Business 17, can be frustrating to navigate, especially in the summer season when families flock here and the road seems more like a parking lot (Myrtle's most crowded period is 4th of July week). All of Myrtle's major arteries parallel the Atlantic Ocean. Here's the lowdown on Myrtle's main beach roads:
Ocean Boulevard (Rte. 73) runs right along the Atlantic from Myrtle Beach State Park to 79th Avenue North.

Dogs on the Beach
In Myrtle Beach, no animals are allowed on the beach or on Ocean Boulevard from 13th Avenue South to 21st Avenue North at any time of the year. From mid-May to Labor Day, dogs are allowed on the beach only before 10am and after 5pm (rest of the year any time). Dogs must be leashed at all times in public. Pet owners are responsible for picking up after their pets.

MUST KNOW

Swimming Safely

Be sure to pay attention to beach safety flags posted on the beach: yellow means there's a lifeguard on duty; blue means it's dangerous to swim; red means no swimming allowed. Always swim with a buddy. If you encounter a riptide—a strong current that can sweep you out to sea as fast as 3- to 6mph—don't try to fight it. Immediately yell for help. If help doesn't come right away, stay relaxed and swim parallel to the shore until you are free from the current's pull.

Kings Highway, aka Business 17, is the next road to the west. This often-congested thoroughfare branches off US-17 in Murrells Inlet and reconnects with it north of 79th Avenue.

US-17 Bypass is the route to take if you want to avoid the main drag.

Accommodations

For a selection of lodgings, see Must Stay. There is no lack of hotels and motels in Myrtle Beach, but if you plan to stay for a week or more, or if you're traveling with a large family or a group of families, renting a condominium or vacation villa may be the most economical way to go. For a free guide to the Grand Strand, including an extensive listing of available real-estate rentals, contact the Myrtle Beach Area CVB and Welcome Center *(opposite)*. When you book your lodgings, be sure to ask about golf or other special package deals.

Beach Regulations

Lifeguards are on duty on most Grand Strand beaches during the summer months. Swimming is not permitted beyond 50 yards from the beach, or if the water is over your shoulder height.
Here are some more rules and regulations:

♦ Glass containers and open containers of any alcoholic

Myrtle Beach

Myrtle Beach Area Chamber of Commerce

beverage are not permitted on the beach.

♦ It's illegal to drive on the beach or to set off fireworks.

♦ Thong bathing suits are outlawed on Myrtle Beach's public beaches.

♦ It's against the law to cut, break or destroy sea oats, beach grass or sand fencing.

Important Numbers

Emergency (24hrs)   **911**
(Police/Ambulance/Fire)

Police (non-emergency)
Myrtle Beach: 843-918-1382
North Myrtle Beach:
            843-280-5511
Surfside Beach: 843-913-6368
Medical Referral
Grand Strand Regional
Medical Center: 843-692-1052
24-hour Pharmacy
CVS: 1303 38th Ave. North
843-448-4437

SOUTHERN CHARM

Thoughts of the South Carolina Coast inevitably bring to mind palmetto trees and moss-draped live oaks, broad stretches of pale sand, the multitude of amusements of **Myrtle Beach★**, and the handsome city of **Charleston★★★**, where the area's history began.

Anchoring the coast on a narrow peninsula of land where the Ashley and Cooper rivers converge, Charleston was born in 1670 when a group of English colonists landed on the western bank of the Ashley River. The swampy settlement they named Charles Towne (after King Charles II; *see sidebar opposite*) was so plagued by disease and hunger during its first decade that the colonists moved the town in 1680 to a better location on the peninsula across the river. Charles Towne's new location, surrounded on three sides by water, was a natural site for trade. With the influx of settlers from elsewhere in the colonies, as well as from Europe (French Huguenots, English, Irish, Scottish) and Barbados, Charles Towne grew to be the fifth-largest city in colonial America by 1690. A wealthy merchant class supported its bustling port.

To protect its citizens from attack by the Spanish and unfriendly Indians, fortified walls were built around the city in the late 17C along the boundaries of the Cooper River and present-day Meeting Street. By 1717, however, the walls were taken down to make room for the expanding city.

Rice, indigo and cotton thrived along the coast in the Lowcountry's temperate, humid climate, and soon hundreds of plantations,

Fast Facts
♦ In 2011, Charleston was ranked as the Top US City by Conde Nast *Traveler* magazine.
♦ The 14 million visitors to the Myrtle Beach area each year have a choice of 98,600 lodging units.
♦ Charleston boasts the eighth-largest container port in the US, in terms of the value of its international shipments.

Myrtle Beach 1953 (Pavilion Amusement Park in foreground)

©Myrtle Beach Area Chamber of Commerce

East Bay Street, Charleston

©Alan A. Tobey/iStockphoto.com

largely dependent on slave laborers brought from the west coast of Africa, dotted the landscape.

The Civil War, which heard its first shots in Charleston Harbor in the morning hours of April 12, 1861, changed the city forever. By war's end, the once-thriving port had been shelled into a virtual ghost town. As a result of the abolition of slavery and the poverty that besieged the South after the war, the region's plantation economy gradually disintegrated.

Hounded by natural disasters over the years, plucky Charleston has rebuilt itself after repeated fires, hurricanes and earthquakes (the city sits on the second most active fault in the US). To protect its historic structures, Charleston became the first American city to enact a historic zoning ordinance in 1931. Today Charleston is known for its stunning 18C and 19C **architecture★★★**.

In recent decades, the coast has spiffed itself up even more. Charleston opened the South Carolina Aquarium on Aquarium Wharf *(see Musts for Kids)*, and Myrtle Beach has added shopping centers, entertainment venues and amusement parks to its already impressive roster of attractions. Like any gracious Southern lady, the South Carolina Coast always welcomes visitors. Any season is a good one to bask on the area's wide sandy beaches, revel in its historic architecture, and breathe its magnolia-scented air.

The End of the Lord Proprietors

When King Charles II returned from exile in 1661 to assume the English throne, he showed his gratitude to those who had been most loyal to him by naming eight Lord Proprietors and granting to them all the territory now occupied by North Carolina, South Carolina and Georgia.

The Lord Proprietors, however, took little interest in the colonies that were established on their lands. After their overseers failed to send troops to protect Charles Towne from Spanish attack, the colonists revolted. One thing led to another, and in 1721, the reign of the Lord Proprietors ended when South Carolina became a royal colony, under a British governor.

SOUTHERN CHARM

21

HISTORIC DISTRICT

Any visit to Charleston should begin on the lower tip of the 5.2 square-mile peninsula formed by the Ashley and Cooper rivers. This area composes the **Historic District★★★**, the heart of Charleston since 1680. It encompasses the land specified in the original 17C Grand Modell, or city plan. As you stroll the palmetto-studded streets lined with gas lanterns, it's easy to imagine the colonial days when Charleston was London in miniature—a prosperous aristocratic city whose gentry built many of the splendid houses you see today.

Here, you'll discover some of the city's legendary sights and its loveliest structures, along with a multitude of boutiques, antiques shops and restaurants that cater to a wide range of tastes and pocketbooks.

Nathaniel Russell House★★★

51 Meeting St. 843-724-8481. www.historiccharleston.org. Visit by 30-minute guided tour only, year-round Mon–Sat 10am–5pm, Sun 2pm–5pm. Closed Thanksgiving Day & Dec 24–25. $10. Combination tickets are available for Nathaniel Russell and Aiken-Rhett houses.

Touring Tip

If you like historic houses, you can save a few bucks by purchasing a combination ticket ($16) for the Nathaniel Russell and Aiken-Rhett houses, both of which are operated by the Historic Charleston Foundation. **Remember the Children.**

If you just see one historic house in Charleston, make it this one. The sister property to the Aiken-Rhett House, the 3-story, 9-room

Nathaniel Russell House has been restored to its 19C glory after the roof collapsed when Hurricane Hugo blew through town in 1989. The brick residence, considered to be one of the best examples of Federal-style architecture in the US, was built in 1808 for Nathaniel Russell and his wife, Sarah. Born in Rhode Island, Russell came to Charleston at age 27 in 1765, as an agent for a Providence import-export firm. When he moved his family into the new house in 1808, Russell was 70 years old, and ranked as one of the city's wealthiest merchants. You can see his prosperity for yourself in the ornate carved woodwork and moldings, and the collections of fine 18C Charleston-made antiques and English silver that decorate the lovely rooms.

Nathaniel Russell House

©M.Linda Lee/Michelin

Music Room, Nathaniel Russell House

©Bill Struhs/Historic Charleston Foundation

Hey, Honey—Wanna Joggle?

The first thing the tour guide will point out to you at Nathaniel Russell House is the **joggling board**, which looks like a sort of garden seat. You might think it's a children's toy—and indeed, kids throughout the centuries have loved them—but in 19C Charleston, joggling boards were used more often by courting couples. It's said that a home that had a joggling board never had an unmarried daughter. Try it with a friend and see for yourself: as you bounce gently on the board, your partner will slip closer and closer. To get one for your garden, contact the Old Charleston Joggling Board Company *(652 King St.; 843-723-4331; www.oldcharlestonjogglingboard.com)*.

What's Inside?

♦ The Nathaniel Russell House is famed for its **"flying" staircase★★★**—a freestanding spiral that circles up, seemingly unsupported, to the third floor.

♦ Rooms are laid out in identical symmetrical suites—rectangular, oval and square—on each of the three floors.

♦ The oval **Music Room** was used routinely for entertaining Charleston's elite. Resembling windows, the room's large paneled mirrors were intended to reflect the firelight.

What's Outside?

♦ A formal English garden flanks the house with boxwood hedges and plants favored by 19C Charlestonians. An amateur gardener, Mrs. Russell first festooned this "urban plantation" with flowers, myrtle bowers, and lemon and orange trees.

©Historic Charleston Foundation

Garden, Nathaniel Russell House

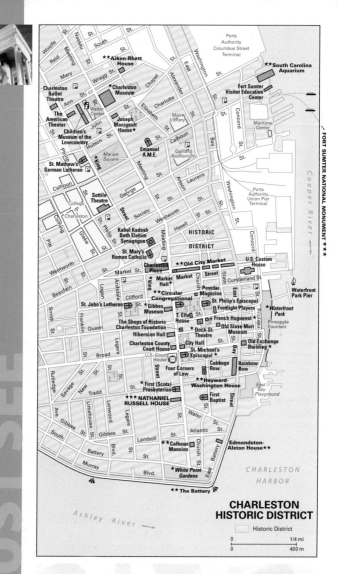

CHARLESTON HISTORIC DISTRICT

Historic District

0 ————— 1/4 mi
0 ————— 400 m

From **The Battery** at the tip of the peninsula north to Calhoun Street and several blocks beyond, the historic district encompasses the city's 18C and 19C mansions, churches, theaters, civic buildings and waterfront facilities. Oak-shaded streets, many made of cobblestone, and pleasant parks punctuate the district.

Aiken-Rhett House

©Historic Charleston Foundation

Aiken-Rhett House★★

48 Elizabeth St. 843-723-1159. www.historiccharleston.org. Visit by 30-minute guided tour only, year-round Mon–Sat 10am–5pm, Sun 2pm–5pm. Closed Thanksgiving Day & Dec 24–25. $10. Combination tickets are available for Aiken-Rhett and Nathaniel Russell houses.

What's the difference between conservation and restoration? The answer will be clear after you visit the Aiken-Rhett House and the **Nathaniel Russell House★★★**, its sister property, both of which are maintained by the Historic Charleston Foundation. Unlike other Charleston historic houses

that have been restored to their former elegance, the 12-room Aiken-Rhett House has been preserved as it appeared c.1860, just before the outbreak of the Civil War.

Built as a Federal-style brick double house *(see sidebar below)* in 1817, the house was purchased in 1827 by wealthy cotton merchant William Aiken Sr.

After his death, his only son, William Jr., inherited the house with his wife, Harriet. The new owners made significant changes to the structure, moving the front entrance, building a large addition, and reconfiguring the first floor with an arched marble entry-hall staircase, gracious double parlors

The Single House

As you wander through the historic district, you'll notice narrow houses where the porch faces the side instead of the street. This type of dwelling is known as a single house, Charleston's distinctive contribution to American architecture, which is based on a typical West Indian design (many of Charleston's early settlers were planters from Barbados). The typical single house is one room wide and two rooms deep, and includes a long piazza—the Charlestonian term for the airy porches designed to catch prevailing breezes—lying behind a false front door on the narrow side of the house that opens onto the street. The real entrance to the house is off the piazza. A variation on this theme, the **double house** is a near square house with a room in each corner, divided by a central hall.

HISTORIC DISTRICT

25

The Last Big One: Hurricane Hugo

On September 21, 1989, a category-four hurricane by the name of Hugo slammed into the South Carolina coast, bringing winds of up to 135mph and a storm surge of 20 feet—the highest tidal surge ever recorded in the state. Although the barrier islands suffered the brunt of the storm, in downtown Charleston 60 buildings were flattened, 5,100 houses were destroyed, and nearly 12,000 homes were left uninhabitable after the tempest passed. In addition to a death toll of 26 people in South Carolina, Hurricane Hugo racked up a whopping $7.2 billion worth of damage.

Outbuilding, Aiken-Rhett House

©Terry Richardson/Historic Charleston Foundation

into her bedroom and closed off several rooms, furnishings and all. After Harriet's death, her daughter did little to maintain the house, except to add electricity to several of the rooms. When the Historic Charleston Foundation acquired the crumbling property in 1995, they opted to clean, stabilize and preserve it, just as they'd found it.

and an art gallery. The couple returned from travels in Europe with fine paintings and sumptuous furnishings, some of which can still be seen in the house.

Aiken, who served as governor of South Carolina from 1844 to 1846, was a well-to-do rice planter. He died in 1887. After his death, Harriet converted the ballroom

Interior – Today, the eerie ravages of time are evident in the rooms, especially in the occasional pieces of original furniture with their tattered fabric, and in the peeling wallpaper—but that's all part of the property's charm.

Grounds – Out back, the original 1817 outbuildings (typical of every 19C town house in Charleston)

The High Battery

©Ron Rocz/Historic Charleston Foundation

MUST SEE

East Battery

©Janette Siler/Michelin

include the slaves' quarters, kitchen and stables.

The Battery★★

If you've seen any photographs at all of Charleston, chances are you've seen the Battery—it figures prominently on almost every advertisement for the city (and on every other souvenir you'll find in town). Indeed, this historic district landmark defines the tip of Charleston's peninsula.

Long considered a strategic point from which to defend the city, the Battery takes its nickname from its military service.

The site is protected by a high seawall that lines the Cooper River side of Charleston Harbor; this wall replaced the masonry structure built in 1700 to fortify the city. Strengthened over the years to ward off hurricanes—including Hurricane Hugo in 1989—the wall became known as the High Battery for the gun emplacement stationed here during the War of 1812. Earthen batteries were constructed during the Civil War, although they never saw much action. After the war ended in 1865, the Battery reverted to more peaceful uses as a park, now graced with statues, fountains, trees and plantings.

What's Not To Like About The Battery?

Views★★★ – Walkers, joggers and hosts of visitors frequent the pretty oleander-lined promenade to savor **views★★★** of the Cooper River to the east and Charleston Harbor to the south. The graceful mansions that line the East and South Battery (depending on which side of the corner they're located) are time-tested dowagers that have withstood many a storm. Views stretch out over the water to distant Fort Sumter (with flagpole) and Sullivans Island.

Architecture★★★ – The elegant pastel-painted mansions set along the Battery, positioned so that their airy piazzas catch the prevailing breezes off the river, provide stellar examples of Charleston's noted antebellum residential architecture.

White Point Gardens★ –
See Parks and Gardens.
At the seaside corner of East Bay Street, the lovely green space is named for the mounds of sun-

bleached oyster shells that once accumulated here.

Calhoun Mansion★★

16 Meeting St. 843-722-8205. www.calhounmansion.net. Visit by 30-minute guided tour only, Mar–Nov daily 11am–5:30pm (last tour 5pm). Rest of the year daily 11am–5pm (last tour 4:30pm). Closed Thanksgiving Day & Dec 25. $15. Grand Tour (1hr 30min) of entire mansion by reservation; $50.

With 24,000 square feet of living space, the 3-story Calhoun Mansion ranks as Charleston's largest single residence. Built in 1876 in the Italianate style for wealthy banker George Williams, the home was designed by Virginia architect W. P. Russell. Upon Williams' death in 1903, the house passed to his daughter Sarah and her husband, Patrick Calhoun (grandson of statesman John C. Calhoun). In 1910 it was remodeled by Louis Comfort Tiffany. Now a private residence, the home is filled with the owner's furnishings, paintings and sculpture collected around the world. The mansion encompasses

35 rooms, many of which retain the exquisite original satinwood, black walnut and chestnut woodwork; Minton tiles; and ornate gasoliers. Two floors are seen on the tour.

What's Inside?

+ The **Main Hallway** holds the sole piece of furniture belonging to George Williams: the 24-seat dining table (displayed without its leaves).
+ The **Reception Room**, richly appointed, features window cornices original to the house.
+ The airy second-floor **Music Room** rises 35 feet to a large glass skylight in the coved ceiling painted by Louis Tiffany.

What's Outside?

+ The highlight of the gardens is the **Southern Garden** with its boxwood ring encircling 15 rounded hedges. The center-piece is a 19C statue of Mercury.
+ The **Eastern Garden** features a central fountain symmetrically flanked by koi ponds underlaid with intricate brickwork.
+ At the rear of the house, the elaborate **Japanese Gardens**

Calhoun Mansion

MUST SEE

Japanese Gardens, Calhoun Mansion

©Gwen Cannon/Michelin

William Alston, whose son, Charles, added the third-floor piazza and other Greek Revival details, when he lived in the house.

A tour of the exquisitely decorated mansion, with its three airy piazzas supported by Doric and Corinthian columns, depicts the life of Charleston's 19C elite. Here you'll find Alston family furnishings, silver, and a collection of more than 1,000 rare volumes in Charles Alston's second-floor library.

are adorned with a large main fountain and a columned archway wrapped with Japanese wisteria.

♦ Ornate iron gates and fencing that incorporates a rope pattern are original to the property.

Edmondston-Alston House★★

21 East Battery. 843-722-7171. www.edmonstonalston.com. Visit by 30-minute guided tour only, year-round Tue–Sat 10am–4:30pm, Sun & Mon 1pm–4:30pm. Closed Thanksgiving Day & Dec 25. $10.

Imagine what tales this stunning house could tell, overlooking the harbor as it has since 1825, when it was built for Scotsman and cotton trader Charles Edmondston as the first house on the High Battery. When the cotton market turned sour 13 years later, Edmondston sold the property to moneyed Charleston rice planter Colonel

Edmondston-Alston House

©Middleton Place, Charleston, South Carolina

Heyward-Washington House★★

87 Church St. 843-722-2996. www.charlestonmuseum.org. Visit by 30-minute guided tour only, year-round Mon–Sat 10am–5pm, Sun 1pm–5pm. Closed major holidays. $10. Combination ticket ($22) available for Heyward-Washington House, Joseph Manigault House and the Charleston Museum.

21 East Battery Bed & Breakfast

21 East Battery. 843-556-0500 or 888-721-7488. www.21eastbattery.com. Rates range from $295–$435, depending on the season. You may not be able to spend the night in the Edmondston-Alston House, but you can stay on the grounds of this urban complex in Charles Edmonston's 1825 carriage house. Now a B&B, the inn offers guests a choice of three rooms with private baths. Rates include a gourmet breakfast and a complimentary tour of the Edmondston-Alston House.

HISTORIC DISTRICT

Named for Thomas Heyward, its original owner, this redbrick double house remains structurally unchanged from 1772 when it was built within the boundaries of the old walled city. George Washington slept here during a visit to Charleston in 1791—thus the second part of the home's name. Heyward distinguished himself as a signer of the Declaration of Independence, as a criminal court judge and as an officer in the South Carolina militia during the Revolution. A tour of his home gives you a first-hand glimpse at the luxuries a man of his status enjoyed in colonial Charleston. Outside, you can see the original kitchen, and a formal garden containing symmetrical plots of camellias, tea olives, boxwood, roses and herbs—all plants

Example from the Furniture Collection.

©Charleston Museum

introduced to the Lowcountry before 1791.

Furniture Collection★ – Inside, the rooms are decorated with a fine collection of 18C Charleston-made furniture, including the priceless Holmes bookcase—which survived British mortar fire during the Revolutionary War—as well as pieces attributed to cabinetmaker Thomas Elfe *(see below)*.

Old City Market★★

On Market St. between Meeting & E. Bay Sts.

A trip to Charleston just isn't complete without a stroll through the Old City Market. Stretching from Meeting Street to the river along Market Street, the three-

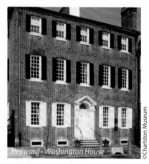

Heyward - Washington House

©Charleston Museum

Thomas Elfe

Born in England, Thomas Elfe emigrated to Charles Towne in 1747 and established himself as a tradesman in the thriving city. His skill soon made him one of the most sought-after cabinetmakers in the area, and a wealthy man in his day. Inspired by his contemporary Thomas Chippendale, Elfe made more than 1,500 pieces between 1768 and his death in 1775, including beds, chairs, bookcases and desks. In addition to the Heyward-Washington House, you can see Elfe's pieces in the **Thomas Elfe House**, set up as it was when he lived there in the mid-18C *(54 Queen St.; 843-722-9161; www.thomaselfehouse.com; visit by 30-minute guided tour only, year-round Mon–Fri 10am–noon; $8).*

MUST SEE

block-long row of open-air sheds with arched openings fills daily with vendors selling everything from sweetgrass baskets to T-shirts *(see Shopping)*. The site where the stalls now stand used to be marshland belonging to the Pinckney family *(see Plantations)*, who donated it for use as a city market in the late 1700s. At the turn of the 19C, the swampy plot was filled in to create a meat and produce market. For years, the market served as the commercial hub of the city.

Market Hall★ – *Market St. at Meeting St.* You'll know you're at the market when you see the elegant 1841 Greek Revival landmark that stands like a sentinel in front of the market sheds. Designed by local architect Edward Brickell White, Market Hall resembles a Roman temple. The structure was restored to its 19C grandeur—to the tune of $3.6 million—after sustaining severe damage during Hurricane Hugo in 1989. Although Market Hall's exterior may look like stone, it's really made from brick covered with stucco scored to resemble stone blocks; the brownstone steps

Market Hall
©M.Linda Lee/Michelin

and trim take on a reddish hue in the sunlight. A recent renovation enclosed and air-conditioned the Great Hall. Sheep and bull skulls on the stucco frieze refer to the 19C meat market that once stood here.

Confederate Museum – Market Hall now houses a substantial collection of Civil War memorabilia on its second floor *(see Museums)*.

Dock Street Theatre★

135 Church St., at Queen St. 843-577-7183. www.charleston stage.com.

Above its recessed porch lined with brownstone columns, this Church Street fixture features a lacy wrought-iron balcony, which looks like something you'd see

©Gwen Cannon/Michelin
Old City Market

Dock Street Theatre

new dressing rooms and elevators, upgraded wiring and lighting, and seismic reinforcements. Since reopening in spring of 2010, the refurbished theater once again hosts the Spoleto USA Festival and other events and continues to serve as the home of the Charleston Stage Company *(see Performing Arts)*.

Joseph Manigault House★

350 Meeting St., at the corner of John St. 843-722-2996. www.charlestonmuseum.org. Visit by 30-minute guided tour only, year-round Mon–Sat 10am–5pm, Sun 1pm–5pm. Closed major holidays. $10. Combination tickets are available for Heyward-Washington House, Joseph Manigault House and the Charleston Museum ($22).

in the French Quarter of New Orleans. The original "theatre in Dock Street" opened in 1736, the first structure in the American colonies dedicated solely to the performing arts. The current building, constructed as a hotel in 1809, is the fourth structure on this site. In the 1930s it was renovated as part of a WPA project to function again as a theater. After 70 years of continuous use, the 464-seat theater, which is owned by the city, recently underwent a multimillion-dollar renovation that restored its historic character and included

Gentleman-architect Gabriel Manigault designed this graceful three-story brick residence, with its distinctive half-moon-shaped piazza (north side), for his brother Joseph in 1803. Located just across from the Charleston Museum (and the Visitor Center), the house captures the lifestyle of prosperous early-19C Huguenot rice planters. Typical of the Adam (or Federal) style of architecture—named for English architect Robert Adam—the mansion incorporates a variety of shapes, such as arched doorways, a sinuous **staircase★★**, and fanlights. Throughout the residence, you'll see delicately carved woodwork, another earmark of the Adam style, as well as a group of French, English and American 19C furniture from the Charleston Museum's fine collection.

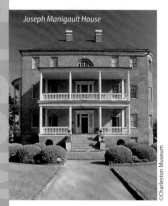

Joseph Manigault House

MUST SEE

Elegant staircase in Joseph Manigault House

©Charleston Museum

Old Exchange Building★

122 E. Bay St., at Broad St. 843-727-2165. www.oldexchange.org. Open year-round daily 9am–5pm. Closed Jan 1, Thanksgiving Day & Dec 25. $8.

The Old Exchange Building was the city's commercial, political and social hub in the late 18C. Constructed in 1771 on the site of Half-Moon Bastion—part of the original fortifications around the city—the Georgian-style Exchange and Custom House, with its arched Palladian windows and distinctive cupola, was the last structure that the British erected in Charleston. Soon after its completion, the Exchange received George Washington himself, who visited Charleston in May 1771. An elaborate dinner was served to him in the 4,000-square-foot first-floor arcade, followed by a grand ball. The Exchange is one of only three buildings in the country where the US Constitution was ratified in 1788 (the other two were Independence Hall in Philadelphia and Faneuil Hall in Boston). Some of the very men who signed the document had been imprisoned downstairs in the damp, gloomy Provost Dungeon during the British occupation of the city. Displays inside detail the

The Charleston Tea Party

Sure, you've heard of the Boston Tea Party, but did you know there was a similar incident in Charleston? There was no dumping of tea into the harbor here, but Patriots did attempt to seize a shipment of 256 chests of East India Company tea from Britain. They were protesting the fact that the British government authorized the company to export tea without paying the usual customs duties, thus giving them an unfair advantage over colonial merchants. After meeting with the colonists, representatives of the East India Company agreed not to accept shipment of the tea, and customs officials took possession of the goods for non-payment of duties. The chests were stored in the Exchange warehouse until the Revolution broke out in 1776, at which time the confiscated tea was sold to raise money for the colonial army. How's that for an ironic twist?

Old Exchange Building

building's history, especially its connection to America's fight for independence.

Provost Dungeon – *Visit by 20-minute guided tour only.* Kids will enjoy the tour of the spooky dungeon, constructed of brick in 1781 with a barrel-vaulted ceiling and thick columns. Restored in 1965, the building was opened as a museum in 1966.

Today it is outfitted with animatronic figures representing characters from the city's past, who tell their woeful tales. Some prominent citizens were held here, charged by the British with giving intelligence to the Patriots. This is the one place in town where you can see part of the **original seawall** built in the late 17C to fortify the city.

Preserving the Past

Ravaged by the Civil War and the ensuing years of Reconstruction, Charleston by the 1920s was a shadow of its former self. With its economy faltering, the city had no money to fix up its grand colonial and antebellum houses, many of which were literally crumbling with age and neglect. Charlestonians at the time were, as they put it, "too poor to paint, too proud to whitewash."

Spurred partly by the cultural re-awakening of the Charleston Renaissance *(see p 76)*, Charleston in 1931 became the first city in America to enact a major preservation ordinance. Thanks to the efforts of **The Historic Charleston Foundation**, founded in 1947 to "preserve and protect the integrity of Charleston's architectural, historical and cultural heritage," and other preservation organizations, today Charleston's restored antebellum residential **architecture★★★** ranks among the best in the country.

Stop in at **The Shops of Historic Charleston Foundation** *(108 Meeting St.; see Shopping)*, where you can pick up a copy of the Historic District walking-tour booklet. There's also a good display there explaining the mix of architectural styles you'll find in Charleston.

MUST SEE

Hibernian Hall

105 Meeting St.
Not open to the public.

Built in 1840, this National Historic Landmark was—and still is—the meeting place for the Ancient Order of Hibernians, an Irish Catholic organization whose members are devoted to the welfare of their fellow Irishmen. Hibernian Hall's claim to historical fame is the fact that it hosted the National Democratic Convention of 1860 for the party faction supporting Stephen A. Douglas to run against Abraham Lincoln (and we all know who won that vote). The hall is pure Greek Revival in style, designed by Philadelphia architect Thomas U. Walter, whose work includes an expansion of the Capitol in Washington, DC. Notice the harp carved above the main door and incorporated into the iron entrance gate; this motif echoes the Irish heritage of the hall's founders.

Hibernian Hall
©Doug Rogers/Michelin

Old Slave Mart Museum

6 Chalmers St. 843-958-6467.
www.oldslavemart.org. Open
year-round Mon–Sat 9am–5pm.
Closed Jan 1, Thanksgiving Day &
Dec 25. $7.

Tucked away on a residential street, this former slave mart opened in 1856 when the practice of selling slaves publicly on the side of the Custom House (now the Old Exchange Building) was outlawed. Charleston had become a key site in the domestic slave-selling system. The last auction was held here in 1863.
In 1938 the building was opened as a museum showcasing African

Four Corners of Law

Originally intended to be a grand public square, the intersection of Broad and Meeting streets holds public buildings on its four corners that each represent a different branch of the law:

- Completed in 1788, the **Charleston County Court House**, on the northwest corner, exemplifies state law.
- The 1896 Renaissance Revival **U.S. Court House and Post Office**, on the southwest corner, represents federal law.
- On the northeast corner, Palladian-style **City Hall**, built in 1801, stands in for municipal law.
- **St. Michael's Episcopal Church★**, which graces the southeast corner, represents God's law *(see Historic Sites).*

arts and crafts, and operated until 1987, when the city took over the property. Renovated and reopened in 2007, the museum retains the high-arched entrance of the original mart, which once featured octagonal pillars and an iron gate. Exhibits in the large ground-floor room, which served as the salesroom, focus on the slave trade in Charleston and include slave badges, leg shackles and other artifacts.

Powder Magazine

79 Cumberland St. 843-722-9350. Open year-round Mon–Sat 10am–4pm, Sun 1pm–4pm. $3.

Powder Magazine

©Doug Rogers/Michelin

Understandably, there are few structures that survive today from the days when Charleston was the domain of the Lord Proprietors appointed by King Charles II. The windowless, tile-roof Powder Magazine, completed in 1713, is one of them.

Inside its 32-inch-thick walls, soldiers stored munitions and gunpowder used to defend the fortified city against attack from Spanish troops, hostile Indians and marauding pirates. (The cannons out front aren't quite that old, though; they date from the Revolutionary War.) It's worth a walk through the oldest public building in the city, where an interactive exhibit tells the story of Charleston's earliest days.

U.S. Custom House

200 E. Bay St.
Not open to the public.

The stately white United States Custom House lords it over East Bay Street at the foot of Market Street. Shaped in a cross, the monumental structure sports massive Corinthian columns and measures 259 feet on its east-west axis and 152 feet on

Keeper of the Gates

In Charleston's Historic District, the wrought- and cast-ironwork that adorns many of the garden gates rivals New Orleans in this decorative art form, which evolved from 19C plantation blacksmiths who made and repaired tools. The best examples of this art were fashioned by Charleston's favorite son, **Philip Simmons** (1912–2009), known world-wide for his decorative ironwork. Simmons was born on nearby Daniel Island; his work appears in some 500 gates, balconies and fences throughout the district. In 1982 Simmons was named a National Folk Treasure by the Smithsonian and the National Park Service when one of his gates was displayed at the Smithsonian Institution's National Museum of American History in Washington, DC. After his death at age 97, his home was turned into a museum *(30 1/2 Blake St.; 843-723-1259; call for hours; www.philipsimmons.us).*

U.S. Custom House

its north-south axis. Construction began in 1853, but engineering problems, lack of funding, and damage caused by the intervening Civil War delayed its completion until 1879. Ever since then, it has operated as a United States Customs facility.

Rows of Row Houses

Rainbow Row – *79–107 E. Bay St.* A favorite Charleston photo subject, the bright multicolored row of colonial town houses reigns as the largest intact cluster of Georgian row houses in the US. The earliest of these dwellings, which were built as merchants' residences, dates to 1740.

Cabbage Row – *89–91 Church St.* In the 1920s, poor black residents of this late-18C double tenement used to sell vegetables from their windowsills, thus giving the site its nickname. These residences provided the inspiration for "Catfish Row" in Dubose Heyward's 1925 novel, *Porgy*. Heyward's story became the basis for George Gershwin's folk opera *Porgy and Bess*, a fictional look at black life in 1920s Charleston. Today the dwellings are filled with shops.

Rainbow Row

HISTORIC SITES

Since its founding in 1670, Charleston has witnessed some very momentous events. The first great victory of the Revolution was won here at Fort Moultrie in 1776, and the first shots of the Civil War were fired in Charleston Harbor in 1861. More recently, in 2000, the Civil War-era submarine *H.L. Hunley* was raised from the depths of the harbor. But don't just read about it—come discover Charleston's fascinating history for yourself.

Fort Sumter National Monument★★★

Accessible only by boat from Patriots Point or the Fort Sumter Visitor Education Center, located on Liberty Square (next to the aquarium at the east end of Calhoun St.). 843-883-3123. www.nps.gov/fosu. Open mid-Mar–mid-Aug 10am–5:30pm; rest of the year, call for hours. Closed Jan 1, Thanksgiving Day & Dec 25. Fee for cruise includes admission to fort (see sidebar on next page).

Imagine this lonely outpost at the entrance to Charleston Harbor alive with cannon fire, men running and shouting, the powder magazines exploding in flames. This was the scene on April 12, 1861, when Confederate forces fired the first shots of the Civil War.

When South Carolina seceded from the Union on December 20, 1860, four forts guarded the entrance to Charleston Harbor: Fort Sumter on its manmade island, Fort Moultrie on Sullivans Island, Fort Johnson on James Island, and Castle Pinckney on Shutes Folly Island. The five-sided brick fort, named for South Carolina Revolutionary War hero Thomas Sumter, was 90 percent complete at the time, but only 15

Fort Facts

- ◆ It took seven million bricks to build Fort Sumter.
- ◆ Outer walls were five feet thick.
- ◆ The fort's three tiers rose 50 feet above water level.
- ◆ Designed for a garrison of 650 men, the fort could bear an armament of 135 guns.

Fort Sumter National Monument

Courtesy of the National Park Service

Fort Sumter ruins

of the fort's more than 100 cannons stood mounted and ready.

On December 26, Union major Robert Anderson secretly relocated his cadre of 85 men from Fort Moultrie to Fort Sumter—a move that South Carolina responded to by demanding the evacuation of Charleston Harbor by U.S. Government forces. Over the ensuing months, government attempts to resupply the fort led to increasing tensions between the North and South.

A final government effort to get supplies through to Sumter in April 1861 prompted General P.G.T. Beauregard, commander of the Confederate troops in Charleston, to ask Major Anderson to surrender the stronghold. When Anderson refused, Confederate officers informed him that their forces would open fire in an hour. At 3:30am on April 12, 1861, Rebels fired on Sumter. The cannonade continued for 34 hours, until Major Anderson finally surrendered the fort on April 13.

"The firing of the mortar woke the echoes from every nook and corner of the harbour…," wrote Stephen Lee, aide-de-camp to General Beauregard, who commanded the Confederate forces.

"A thrill went through the whole city. It was felt that the Rubicon was passed…."

After the Civil War ended in 1865, Fort Sumter stood neglected until 1898, when it was used during the Spanish-American War. The fort was decommissioned in 1947 and transferred to the National Park Service the following year.

Getting to the Fort

SpiritLine Cruises offers the only authorized boat transportation to Fort Sumter. Boats depart from the **Fort Sumter Visitor Education Center** on Liberty Square, and from **Patriots Point Naval Maritime Museum** *(see Musts for Kids)* in Mt. Pleasant. On the 30-minute narrated cruise, you'll learn about events leading to the war. *Allow 2hrs to visit the fort, including the boat trip.* For boat schedules, 843-881-7337 or 800-789-3678. www.fortsumtertours.com. $17 adults, $10 children (children under age 6 ride free).

HISTORIC SITES

Palmetto Flag, Palmetto State

Why is South Carolina's state flag decorated with a palmetto tree? The design derives from the one that graced the flag carried by South Carolina's Palmetto Guard. Members of the unit planted this standard on Fort Sumter's parapet in April 1861, when Confederate troops took Fort Sumter. Adopted in January 1861, the flag bears a palmetto tree to honor the soft palmetto logs that absorbed enemy shells and saved Fort Moultrie from British attack in 1776. Since 1861, South Carolina has been known as the Palmetto State.

Visiting Fort Sumter

Fort Sumter Visitor Education Center – *Next to the aquarium at the east end of Calhoun St. Open daily 8:30am–5pm. Closed Jan 1, Thanksgiving Day & Dec 25.*
This is the place to purchase tickets for the boat trip to the fort. Displays detail the events leading up to the first shots of the Civil War. Artifacts here include Major Anderson's original garrison flag that waved over Fort Sumter.

Fort Walking Tour – Once at the fort, you can inspect the casemates and the ruins of the barracks and officers' quarters on the self-guided walking tour. A **museum** in Battery Huger, added in 1899, tells the story of the fort and its role in the Civil War through informative panels, armaments and artifacts.

Fort Moultrie★

1214 Middle St., on Sullivans Island. 9mi northeast of Charleston via US-17 North & Rte. 703. 843-883-3123. www.nps.gov/fosu/historyculture/ fort_moultrie.htm. Open year-round daily 9am–5pm. Closed Jan 1, Thanksgiving Day & Dec 25. $3 (ages 16 & under free).

What's in a fort? In this case, wood and sand. Hastily built with wood from abundant local palmetto trees, the first fort on Sullivans Island was constructed in 1776 to protect Charleston from British attack. Soon afterward, Fort Moultrie gained fame as the crude rampart that held off the British during the battle for Sullivans Island. Soft palmetto logs that formed the walls of the early fort helped thwart the Redcoats' attack

Fort Moultrie

by absorbing the British shells. After the battle, the palmetto tree was adopted as the South Carolina state symbol.

In 1794 Fort Moultrie was rebuilt as a five-sided battlement with earth and timber walls; this version was destroyed by a hurricane in 1804. The third incarnation of the fort—and the one you see here now—arose in 1809, and saw action through World War II. Fort Moultrie was decommissioned in 1947, the same year as Fort Sumter. As you walk through the fort today, you'll find remains from every period of its long history:

- The site of the first fort
- Cannon Walk, with its Civil War artillery
- Two batteries that defended the harbor from 1898 on
- World War II Control Post

Outside the fort's Sally Port lie the graves of the Seminole leader Osceola, who died here in 1838, and 5 of the 62 crewman who died when the US warship *Patapsco* was sunk in nearby waters in 1965.

Charles Towne Landing State Historic Site

1500 Old Towne Rd., 3mi northwest of Charleston via US-17 to Rte. 171. 843-852-4200. www.charlestowne. org. Open year-round daily 9am– 5pm. Closed Dec 24 & 25. $7.50 adults, $3.50 children (ages 6-15).

History comes alive at Charles Towne Landing, on the very spot where the first English colonists landed in 1670. Here, they built a fort on Old Towne Creek and planted the fields with wheat, oranges, tobacco and other crops. Named Charles Towne, for King Charles II of England, the

Charles Towne Landing State Historic Site
©Gwen Cannon/Michelin

settlement lasted only 10 years in these swampy, mosquito-infested lands along the river. Plagued by disease and hunger, the colonists moved the town site across the river to the Charleston peninsula in 1680. Experience early colonial life and explore the ruins of the first settlement, including a reconstruction of the original palisade wall. You'll see archaeology in action here, as scientists constantly uncover the site's hidden past.

Visitor Center – Opened in 2006, the striking visitor center houses a gift shop and a 12-room interactive museum with exhibits on the voyage, the people and the settlement of Charles Towne. A digital dig showcases the archaeological process and on-site discoveries.

Trails and Gardens – Walk the self-guided history trail, with an MP3 player as your audio guide. Also here are 80 acres of gardens, including an Experimental Crop

41

Fickle Finger of Fate

Known as the Merry Monarch, King Charles II returned from exile in 1661 to assume his throne. To reward those who had been most loyal to him, the King granted all the territory now occupied by North Carolina, South Carolina and Georgia to eight Lord Proprietors—aristocrats bearing titles of Duke, Earl or Sir, for the most part. In an interesting bit of historic irony, the Ashley and Cooper rivers in Charleston are named for one of the Lord Proprietors, Anthony Ashley Cooper, Earl of Shaftesbury, who was later imprisoned for plotting against his benefactor, King Charles himself.

Garden showcasing crops—indigo, rice, sugarcane, cotton—the settlers tried to grow here.

Animal Forest – Observe the creatures the settlers met here. *See Musts for Kids.*

The Adventure – Admire this full-size replica of a 17C trading vessel. *See Musts for Kids.*

Legare-Waring House – The former home of philanthropist Ferdinanda Isabella Legare Backer Waring is open only as a special-events venue.

The Citadel

171 Moultrie St. 843-225-3294. www.citadel.edu. The campus is open to visitors daily 8am–6pm.

Rising northwest of the historic district along the Ashley River,

the white Moorish-style notched walls of the Citadel buildings surround green Summerall Field. This well-known military academy began in 1829 as an arsenal and guardhouse to protect the city of Charleston. At that time, the Citadel was located on Marion Square *(Calhoun & Meeting Sts.)* in what is now "downtown" Charleston (the original building, now painted pink, remains on the square as an Embassy Suites hotel). In 1842 the Citadel, along with the Arsenal in Columbia, South Carolina, was converted into the South Carolina Military Academy.

The academy remained on Marion Square until 1910, when it acquired the 200-acre campus on which it's now located.

Touring the Campus – Cadet-led tours of the campus are available during the school year *(to arrange*

The Citadel

Military Dress Parade

If you're into pomp and circumstance, visit on Friday afternoon at 3:45pm during the college year to see the cadets march across central Summerall Field in their crisp full-dress uniforms. Afterwards, you can stop by the Citadel gift shop and pick up a souvenir.

a guided tour, call 843-953-5230). If you want to explore on your own, you can pick up a walking-tour brochure at the museum, and hit the major points of interest. In addition to those sites listed below, several monuments on the grounds honor the heroism of Citadel graduates.

- Gothic-style Summerall Chapel is a popular venue for cadet weddings.
- Mark Clark Grave is the burial place of General Mark W. Clark, former president of the Citadel and one of the top five American military commanders of World War II.
- The 90-foot-high Thomas Dry Howie Carillon Tower rings out concerts with its 59 Dutch bells.
- Inside Daniel Library, the Citadel Murals illustrate the academy's history.

The Citadel Museum – *Just inside the Lesesne Gate on the right (access via Moultrie St.). 3rd floor. 843-953-6846. www.citadel.edu/museum. Open year-round daily noon–5pm. Closed college breaks & major holidays.* See what it's like to be a cadet at the Military College of South Carolina. In this small museum, historic photos, uniforms, weapons, medals and other artifacts tell the story of the Citadel, from its founding in 1842 to its

involvement in today's military operations around the world.

The H.L. Hunley

Located on Charleston's former Naval Base. From I-26, take Exit 216B/Cosgrove Ave. North. 843-743-4865. www.hunley.org. Visit by 30-minute guided tour only, year-round Sat 10am–5pm & Sun noon–5pm. Closed holiday weekends. $12 (free to children under age 5).

Off the coast of Charleston on the night of February 17, 1864, the Confederate submarine *H.L.*

Lt. Dixon's gold coin

Touring Tip

Reservations are not required for the *Hunley* tours, but you can buy tickets in advance by calling 877-448-6539 or online at www.etix.com.

HISTORIC SITES

End of a Journey

The eight-man crew who served aboard the *Hunley* were finally laid to rest on April 17, 2004. Ceremonies began in the morning with a poignant memorial service at White Point Gardens. After the service, a procession led by horse-drawn caissons traveled through the Historic District to Magnolia Cemetery on Charleston Neck *(70 Cunningham Ave.)*, where 2,200 veterans of the Civil War are interred. Here, the crew of the *Hunley* was buried in front of a crowd of thousands of well-wishers, some of whom came from as far away as Australia. If you're interested in visiting the cemetery at night, each October the Confederate Heritage Trust conducts its Ghost Walk by lantern light *(not recommended for young children)*. For information and tickets, call 843-722-8638 or access www.csatrust.org.

Hunley fired a 135-pound torpedo into the Union Navy warship USS *Housatonic*, commanded by Lt. George Dixon, successfully sinking it. The crew on this cylindrical iron boiler, held together with strips of iron and rivets, signaled to shore that they had completed their mission and were on their way back. Then, mysteriously, the sub disappeared.

In 1995, after being lost at sea for 131 years, the *Hunley* was found by adventurer Clive Cussler buried

H.L *Hunley* at Warren Lasch Conservation Center.

in the ocean floor just outside Charleston Harbor. The raising of the *Hunley*, a joint undertaking of the Department of the Navy, the Park Service, Oceaneering International Inc., and Friends of the *Hunley*, was a feat of oceanic proportions. From a platform composed of two massive suction piles (the type used for mooring deepwater oil rigs), engineers lowered a truss onto the sub and positioned nylon slings with inflated foam pillows underneath the craft. On August 8, 2000, a crane lifted the entire truss to the surface and the *Hunley* was placed on a transport barge.

Today scientists in the Warren Lasch Conservation Center in North Charleston are unraveling the mysteries of the *Hunley* and its courageous crew.

You can view the sub in its conservation tank by taking one of the weekend tours.

Historic Churches

Unlike Boston and Philadelphia, which were founded by Puritans and Quakers respectively, Charleston wasn't settled by any one religious group. Although

the Anglican Church of England was predominant in the early city, Charleston promoted religious tolerance, and provided places of worship for many different beliefs. The spires of myriad churches are still visible across the peninsula today, giving rise to Charleston's nickname, "The Holy City." Here are some of the most historic of the peninsula's 180 churches:

Circular Congregational Church★★ – *150 Meeting St.* Designed by Robert Mills, this striking brick Romanesque Revival church stands on the site of the first Independent Church, or Church for Dissenters (non-Anglicans), founded in 1681. The original circular church was built here in 1806; it burned in 1861 and its ruins fell during the 1886 earthquake. The graveyard you see now, the city's oldest, dates to 1695.

Circular Congregational Church

©Doug Rogers/Michelin

First (Scots)
Presbyterian Church

©Doug Rogers/Michelin

was formed in 1731, when 12 Scottish families left the Independent Church and started their own meeting house, the "Scots Kirk." Out front, the wrought-iron gates incorporate a motif of thistles, the symbol of Scotland.

French Huguenot Church★ – *136 Church St.* Seeking to escape religious persecution in France, French Protestants, called Huguenots, came to Charleston beginning in the late 17C. The first church they built was destroyed by fire in 1796. The 1845 church, the third built on this site, was the first Gothic Revival structure in the city; its original pipe organ still provides music during services.

First (Scots) Presbyterian Church★ – *53 Meeting St.* You'll recognize the stucco-covered First Presbyterian Church (1814) by its columned Greek Revival facade and by the twin rounded towers that top its roof. This congregation

St. Michael's Episcopal Church★ – *71 Broad St.* George Washington might not have slept here, but he did worship in this 1761 Colonial-style church. Representing divine law on the intersection known as the **Four Corners of Law** *(see sidebar p 35)*, St. Michael's sits on the site of Charleston's original Anglican Church. Its 186-foot-tall steeple was used as a lookout tower during the

> **Fun Fact**
> The tallest spire (297 feet) in Charleston belongs to **St. Matthew's Lutheran Church** *(405 King St.)*.

French Huguenot Church

©Saskia Damen/Michelin

MUST SEE

St. Philip's Churchyard

The two sections of St. Philip's churchyard (east and west) hold the graves of some of the city's most prominent citizens and historical figures, including South Carolina statesman and secessionist John C. Calhoun, and Edward Rutledge, a signer of the Declaration of Independence.

Revolution, and as a signal tower during the Civil War.

Emanuel A.M.E. Church – *110 Calhoun St.* The oldest Black congregation south of Baltimore, Maryland, attends services at Emanuel African Methodist Episcopal Church. Built in 1891, the Gothic-style church boasts a Victorian interior that retains its original altar, pews and light fixtures.

First Baptist Church – 61 Church St. Designed by Charleston architect Robert Mills, the 1822 First Baptist Church reigns as the oldest Baptist church in the South. The original congregation was organized in Maine in 1692.

Kahal Kadosh Beth Elohim Synagogue – 90 Hassell St. Built in 1840, this impressive Classical Revival-style National Historic Landmark is the second-oldest synagogue in the US, and the oldest one that's still in use. The American Reform Judaism Movement was born here in 1842.

St. John's Lutheran Church – *5 Clifford St.* Charleston's oldest Lutheran congregation dates to 1742, but their first church wasn't completed until 1818. Added in 1859, the steeple with its bell-shaped top may have been the design of Charles Fraser, a Charleston architect and painter.

St. Mary's Roman Catholic Church *– 89 Hassell St.* Organized in 1788, the first Roman Catholic church in the Carolinas and Georgia had a large French congregation; walk through the churchyard and notice that many of the gravestones are in French. The present Classical Revival church building was completed in 1839 to replace a brick building that burned down the previous year.

St. Philip's Episcopal Church – *142 Church St.* Organized in 1680, St. Philip's was founded the year the colonists moved to the peninsula from swampy Charles Towne. The present church dates to 1838; its lofty eight-sided steeple once held a light that guided sailors to Charleston's port.

St. Philip's Episcopal Church

©ExploreCharleston.com

HISTORIC SITES

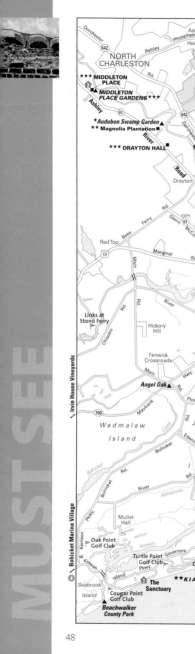

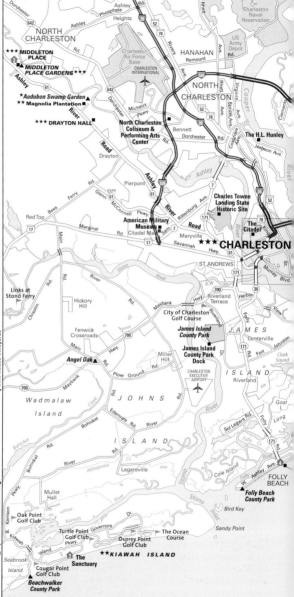

NORTH CHARLESTON

Dorchester Rd.

Ashley Phosphate Rd.

Ashley Heights

★★★ **MIDDLETON PLACE**

MIDDLETON PLACE GARDENS ★★★

★ **Audubon Swamp Garden**

★★ **Magnolia Plantation** ■

★★★ **DRAYTON HALL**

North Charleston Coliseum & Performing Arts Center

Charleston Air Force Base

CHARLESTON INTERNATIONAL

HANAHAN

NORTH CHARLESTON

US Army Depot

■ **The H.L. Hunley**

Charles Towne Landing State Historic Site

American Military Museum

The Citadel

★★★ **CHARLESTON**

ST. ANDREWS

Links at Stono Ferry

City of Charleston Golf Course

Riverland Terrace

James Island County Park

James Island County Park Dock

Angel Oak ▲

CHARLESTON EXECUTIVE AIRPORT

J A M E S

I S L A N D

Centerville

Riverland

J O H N S

I S L A N D

Wadmalaw Island

Legareville

Cole Island

Folly Beach County Park

FOLLY BEACH

Bird Key

Sandy Point

Mullet Hall

Oak Point Golf Club

Turtle Point Golf Club

Osprey Point Golf Club

The Ocean Course

★★ **KIAWAH ISLAND**

The Sanctuary

Cougar Point Golf Club

Beachwalker County Park

Seabrook Island

Bohicket Marina Village

Irvin House Vineyards

48

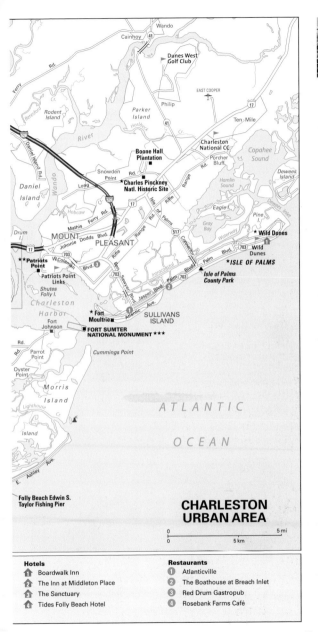

CHARLESTON URBAN AREA

Wando
Cainhoy 41
Dunes West
Golf Club
EAST COOPER 17
Ferry Rd.
Philip 41
Parker Island
Ten Mile
Bereckel Cr.
Rodent Island
River
Harlbed Cr.
Charleston National CC
Boone Hall Plantation
Copahee Sound
526 Daniel Island Rd.
Snowden Point
Porcher Bluff
★ Charles Pinckney Natl. Historic Site
Dewees Island
Daniel Island
Long Rd.
Hamlin Sound
Snowden Point
17
Eagle I.
Pine
Dewees Inlet
Wando
Nabcaw
Mathis Ferry Rd.
Isle of Palms Rd.
Range
Gray Bay
Waterway
★ **Wild Dunes**
Drum I.
MOUNT
Dodds Blvd.
PLEASANT
Range Rd.
517
Connector
Wild Dunes
703
17 703
Johnnie
Rifle
Ben Sawyer Blvd.
★ **ISLE OF PALMS**
★★ **Patriots Point**
W. Coleman
703
Blvd. ③
Jasper Blvd.
Palm Blvd.
703
Palm 703
▲ Isle of Palms County Park
Patriots Point Links
Intracoastal
②
Shutes Folly I.
Atlantic Ave.
①
Charleston Harbor
★ **Fort Moultrie** ■
SULLIVANS ISLAND
Fort Johnson
■ **FORT SUMTER NATIONAL MONUMENT** ★★★
Rd.
Parrot Point
Cummings Point
Oyster Point
Morris Island
Lighthouse Cr.
Island
ATLANTIC

OCEAN

E. Ashley Ave.

Folly Beach Edwin S. Taylor Fishing Pier

CHARLESTON URBAN AREA

0   5 mi
0   5 km

Hotels
🏨 Boardwalk Inn
🏨 The Inn at Middleton Place
🏨 The Sanctuary
🏨 Tides Folly Beach Hotel

Restaurants
① Atlanticville
② The Boathouse at Breach Inlet
③ Red Drum Gastropub
④ Rosebank Farms Café

HISTORIC SITES

49

PLANTATIONS

Shades of Rhett and Scarlett, Charleston's plantations hearken back to an era when rice flourished in flooded land along the rivers, providing riches for plantation owners and exhausting work for their slaves. Meandering up the south side of the Charleston peninsula, the Ashley River served in colonial times as the main route to the stately plantations that lined its banks. By land, an arduous back road traced part of an ancient Cherokee Indian trail. Today, tree-lined **Ashley River Road** *(Route 61)* provides easy access to all but a couple of Charleston's plantations (two lie north of the city in Mt. Pleasant).

How Did Drayton Hall Survive?

No one knows for sure, but the story is that to keep Union troops from destroying the mansion, the slaves remaining at the house put up yellow flags to indicate an outbreak of deadly yellow fever on the site. The Drayton family was divided during the Civil War, with one son fighting for the Union Army and the rest with the Confederate forces. Another theory holds that the son on the Union side used his influence to convince Yankee officers to spare his home. Like their relatives at neighboring Magnolia Plantation, the Draytons weathered the poverty of the Reconstruction years by mining phosphate (used for fertilizer) on their land.

Drayton Hall★★★

3380 Ashley River Rd. 843-769-2600. www.draytonhall.org. Visit by 1-hour guided tour only, year-round daily 9:30am–5pm (last tour at 3:30pm). Closed Jan 1 and Dec 24, 25 & 31. $18.

Considered to be one of the finest existing examples of Georgian-Palladian architecture in America, Drayton Hall is the only plantation house on the Ashley River to have survived the Revolutionary and Civil wars intact. Begun in 1738 and completed in 1742 for John Drayton, the majestic brick mansion—whose architect is unknown—overlooks the river from its 630-acre site. Symmetry

Drayton Hall

©Gwen Cannon/Michelin

Drawing Room, Drayton Hall

©Drayton Hall

and classical detail distinguish the 2-story, 10-room interior, which remains in near original condition. The raised English basement was used largely for storage space. Two 2-story brick outbuildings, known as flankers, were constructed in the 18C, one to serve as a kitchen and the other as a laundry space. One flanker was lost in the 1886 earthquake; the kitchen flanker was destroyed by an 1893 hurricane. Only the privy building, once containing 7 seats, remains from the 18C; it was converted to an office in the late 19C.

Royal Judge John Drayton used his country home for lavish entertaining and as a base from which to manage his other estates.

At his death, Drayton ranked as one of the wealthiest men in the Carolina colony. In 1780 British troops seized the house, which became the headquarters for British commander Sir Henry Clinton, and later for British General Charles Cornwallis; thousands of Redcoats camped on the grounds. The mansion later served as headquarters for the Continental Army during the British occupation of Charleston. The home was occupied by seven generations of the Drayton family before 1969, when it passed into the hands of the National Trust for Historic Preservation, which operates this National Historic Landmark today. A future interpretive center will

To the Manor Born: The Drayton Family

Descended from Norman aristocracy, ancestors of the modern-day Drayton family made their way to England via Aubrey de Vere, who came with William the Conqueror in 1066. After distinguishing himself during the Battle of Hastings, de Vere was awarded a Saxon castle in Northampton, known as Drayton House (de Vere later took the name of this property). The first Draytons to come to America—Thomas and his son, Thomas Jr. *(see Magnolia Plantation, p 54)*—began a long line of that family in the mid-1600s, many of whom became prominent figures in American politics. John Drayton, who built Drayton Hall, was born next door at Magnolia Plantation in 1715.

Mahogany double staircase, Drayton Hall

©Drayton Hall

Touring Tip

If you don't have time to see all parts of the plantation in one visit, you can get a "rain check," which enables you to return free-of-charge on one other day within a seven-day period. You might want to pack a lunch when you come and dine alfresco in one of the lovely picnic areas on the grounds.

showcase pieces in the Drayton Hall furniture collection.

Hall Highlights

Inside, you'll find no furnishings—those were sold at auction long ago—but you will see a wealth of ornate hand-carved and cast-plaster ceilings and hand-carved decorative moldings. The last finished coat of paint on the walls dates to 1885.

- The massive, two-story **portico** on the front side facing the road was reputedly the first of its kind in the colonies.
- Note that the grand **entrance** to Drayton Hall faced the river, since this was how most 18C and 19C guests arrived.
- The 27-foot high entry hall shows off a mahogany **double staircase** with newel posts.
- The Draytons used the upstairs **hall** for formal dining, dances and other social events. Doors here open onto the second story of the portico.
- The downstairs **Drawing Room** boasts a gorgeous ornate ceiling that was hand-molded in wet plaster.

The Plantation Shops at Middleton Place

Looking for some unique gifts to take home? If you just want to shop at Middleton Place, you can do so without paying the site's admission fee. A treasure trove of period reproduction china and silver, Middleton crest glassware, jewelry and more at the Museum Shop includes items handcrafted by the blacksmith, cooper and potter at the plantation's Stableyards. For an everlasting souvenir, stop by the Garden Market & Nursery, where you can choose among 50 varieties of plants—even seedlings from Middleton's famous camellias. Before you head on your way, take a break and have a light snack at the Garden Market.

MUST SEE

Middleton Place★★★

4300 Ashley River Rd. 843-556-6020. www.middletonplace.org. Open year-round daily 9am–5pm. Closed Dec 25. Admission (gardens & grounds) $25 adults, $10 children (free for children under age 6). Combination tickets available for gardens, carriage ride and house tour: $49 adults, $38 children.

The land that came to Englishman Henry Middleton as part of his wife's dowry in 1741 now sweeps down to the Ashley River in 110 acres of green terraced lawns and symmetrical 18C English gardens. Laid out in 1741 by Henry Middleton, the gardens once formed part of the Middleton rice plantation.

Touring Tip

The $25 admission fee takes in all the grounds and gardens, except the house tour, which costs extra ($12). The grounds and gardens are all walkable; if you want to see some areas outside the main plantation grounds, you can take the 45-minute **carriage ride** ($18, in addition to the admission fee).

Middleton Place Restaurant

Open for lunch daily 11am–3pm. Dinner Tue–Thu & Sun 6pm–8pm (Fri–Sat until 9pm). Treat yourself to a meal at airy Middleton Place Restaurant. Classic Southern fare rules the day here; many of the dishes have their origins in colonial times. Starters like peanut soup and okra gumbo both come from recipes brought to the area by African slaves. Lunch entrées range from Southern fried chicken to hickory-smoked pulled pork. You also get a choice of sides like Hoppin' John, collard greens and stone-ground grits, which have a long history in the Lowcountry. All this and a garden view, too—how's that for local color?

Where Do I Begin?

If all this seems like too much to see in one day, make reservations at the Inn at Middleton Place *(see Must Stay).*

Gardens★★★ – The formal 18C English gardens burst into their fullest glory in early spring, but they're worth a visit at any time of year *(see Parks and Gardens).*

©Middleton Place, Charleston, South Carolina

House Museum, Middleton Place

Wood nymph with hydrangeas, Middleton Place

©Middleton Place, Charleston, South Carolina

A Muster of Middletons

The Middleton family exerted their fair share of influence in American politics:

Henry Middleton (1717–1784) – By the time of the Revolution, Henry owned 50,000 acres of land and 800 slaves. He was elected president of the First Continental Congress in 1774. **Arthur Middleton** (1743–1787) – The eldest of Henry's five sons was one of the signers of the Declaration of Independence in 1776.

Henry Middleton (1770–1846) – Henry's grandson and Arthur's eldest son served as governor of South Carolina from 1810 to 1812 and as ambassador to Russia during the 1820s. **Williams Middleton** (1809–1883) – Henry's great-grandson (son of the second Henry) signed the Ordinance of Secession. His staunch support of the Confederate cause spurred Union troops to destroy his family's home in 1865.

House Museum – *Visit by 30-minute guided tour only, Mon noon–4:30pm, Tue–Sun 10am–4:30pm $12.* Built as a gentleman's guest quarters in 1755, this brick dwelling is all that survives of the grand three-building complex that the Middleton family called home. The parts of the complex that weren't destroyed by the Union Army in 1865 toppled in the 1886 earthquake. Inside you'll find a fine collection of family furnishings and memorabilia.

Rice Mill – Positioned at the edge of the rice pond, the brick mill building across from the twin butterfly lakes today houses an exhibit on colonial rice production. Gracing the walls are exquisite watercolors, painted by Alice Ravenel Huger Smith (1876–1958), that illustrate the process.

Stableyards – Visit the stableyards to see what went on behind the scenes on a working colonial plantation. You'll find farm animals here, and artisans who demonstrate such essential skills as weaving, carpentry and blacksmithing.

Magnolia Plantation★★

3550 Ashley River Rd., west of Drayton Hall. 843-571-1266. www.magnoliaplantation.com. Open Mar–Oct daily 8am–5:30pm. Rest of the year daily 8am–4:30pm. $15 adults, $10 children (ages 6-12).

All Aboard!

You could get pretty tired walking around all 500 acres of Magnolia Plantation, which has been managed as a wildlife refuge since 1975. Luckily, there are two other modes of transportation available at Magnolia: the **nature train**, which covers 4 miles of wildlife habitat on the plantation's outskirts; and the electric-powered **nature boat**, which cruises silently along canals that cut through a former rice field. Both offer 45-minute tours *($8)* that are great for spotting wildlife, especially birds. Green-winged teals, red-tailed hawks, Eastern bluebirds and yellow-bellied sapsuckers number among the more than 200 species of birds you might see along the way.

Home to 13 generations of the Drayton family, Magnolia Plantation has been open to the public since shortly after the Civil War, and is still owned by the family that created it. Magnolia's story begins in the mid-1600s, when an Englishman named Stephen Fox left Barbados for Charleston, where he acquired a 500-acre tract of land on the Ashley River (later named Magnolia Plantation). About the same time, Thomas Drayton, another wealthy Barbadian, came to town with his son, Thomas Jr. As it happened, Thomas Jr. ended up marrying Stephen Fox's daughter, Ann, who came with the plantation site as her dowry. Thomas built the original house at Magnolia Plantation, and the Drayton family has operated the estate ever since. In 1820 the estate came into the hands of 22-year-old John Grimke Drayton, who later became a minister. Rev. Drayton developed the striking informal gardens here to comfort his wife, Julia, who was homesick for her native city of Philadelphia.

Gardens – In bloom year-round, Magnolia's 50 acres of gardens are especially stunning in the springtime, when banks of bright azaleas color the grounds. *See Parks and Gardens.*

Plantation House – *Visit by 30-minute guided tour only. $8.* Completed in 1760, the Victorian manor that sits here today is the

Magnolia Plantation

©Magnolia Plantation

Long White Bridge, Magnolia Plantation

©Magnolia Plantation

third dwelling on this site. The first two structures fell victim to fire (the second one was torched by General Sherman's men during the Civil War). After the war, the home you see here today was dismantled and floated down the Ashley River by barge from nearby Summerville. Tour guides highlight early plantation life and point out the many Drayton family heirlooms and the fine collection of early-American antiques that fill the rooms.

Audubon Swamp Garden★ – *$8.* Opened in the 1980s, this 60-acre cypress and tupelo swamp is the most recent addition to the site *(see Parks and Gardens)*.

Charles Pinckney National Historic Site★

1254 Long Point Rd., Mt. Pleasant, 7mi north of Charleston. Take US-17 North and turn left on Long Point Rd.; the historic site sits across the street from Boone Hall. 843-881-5516. www.nps.gov/chpi. Open year-round daily 9am–5pm. Closed Jan 1, Thanksgiving Day & Dec 25.

Patriot and planter Charles Pinckney inherited this Lowcountry estate from his father in 1782. Dubbed Snee Farm, the plantation was Pinckney's favorite "country seat," among the many properties owned by his influential family. Pinckney, who spent much time away from the plantation seeing to affairs of state, was forced to sell the farm in 1817 to settle

Touring Tip

If you're on a budget, note that Snee Farm is the only Charleston area plantation where admission to both the house and grounds is free. Take a few minutes (20, to be exact) to watch the informative video, shown in the cottage, that details the history of Snee Farm and its owner, Charles Pinckney.

Visitor center, Charles Pinckney National Historic Site

his debts. Today only 28 of the property's original 715 acres remain undeveloped. Although no structures are left from the time when the Pinckneys lived here, the one-and-a-half-story cypress and pine cottage illustrates the type of modest, yet comfortable, dwelling built by Lowcountry planters who spent most of their time in their more opulent town houses in Charleston.

Cottage – The rectangular plan, side gable roof and wide front porch of the modest c.1828 home you see here now are all elements shared by 19C coastal cottages.

Charles Pinckney
National Historic Site

Inside, there's no furniture, but informative panels describe Pinckney's life and his career as a statesman, which included three terms as South Carolina governor, one term in the US Senate, and a four-year stint as ambassador to Spain under President Thomas Jefferson.

Grounds – Roam the grounds to discover the archaeological research underway here. To date, scientists have found the vestiges of a detached kitchen, a privy, and a slave village. The latter reveals a wealth of information for anyone interested in the area's African-American heritage.

Boone Hall Plantation

1235 Long Point Rd., Mt. Pleasant. 8mi north of Charleston via US-17 North. Turn left on Long Point Rd.; Boone Hall lies across the street from the Charles Pinckney National Historic Site. 843-884-4371. www.boonehallplantation. com. Open mid-May–Labor Day Mon–Sat 8:30am–6:30pm, Sun

"Constitution Charlie"

An often forgotten founding father and son of a wealthy planter, **Charles Cotesworth Pinckney** (1746–1825) is one of four Charlestonians who went to Philadelphia in May 1787 to help draft the new Constitution of the United States. Prior to leaving, Pinckney and John Rutledge wrote a version of the Constitution, which they later presented to the convention. More than 30 provisions mentioned in "the Pinckney Draught" were incorporated into the final Constitution; these provisions included eliminating religious testing as a qualification for holding public office, assigning impeachment power to the House of Representatives, and establishing a single chief executive. Disliked by James Madison—whose journals provide the best source of information about the convention— the pompous Pinckney never received the credit he deserved for his contributions. Since his personal papers were later destroyed by fire, no records survive today to tell Pinckney's side of the story.

noon–5pm. Rest of the year Mon–Sat 9am–5pm, Sun noon– 5pm. Closed Thanksgiving Day & Dec 25. $19.50.

You'll feel like Scarlett O'Hara as you drive the three-quarter-mile avenue lined by centuries-old moss-draped live oaks leading to Boone Hall (Scarlett would have traveled by horse-drawn carriage). Built in the 1700s, this former cotton plantation is named for Major John Boone, who acquired the 17,000 acres of land in 1681 from the Lord Proprietors of the Carolina colony. Today the remaining 738 acres host visitors and many public and private events; the grounds are a popular film location as well.

Mansion – *Visit by 30-minute guided tour only.* Constructed in 1935, the Colonial Revival-style main house respects the design of the original mid-18C structure, which was destroyed by fire. Guides in hoop skirts take you through the first-floor rooms, pointing out such treasures as the mahogany Hepplewhite dining room table and the English Royal Crown Darby china trimmed in 24-karat gold.

Boone Hall Mansion

©Gwen Cannon/Michelin

Slave cabin at Boone Hall Plantation

Grounds – Located behind the Avenue of the Oaks, you'll find a group of unrestored slave cabins dating back to 1743. The cabins, along with the smokehouse and cotton gin on the grounds, were made with bricks produced on the plantation. The formal gardens contain varieties of antique roses dating back to the 16C.

Boone Hall Farms Market – *2521 US-17, .5mi north of Long Point Rd. 843-856-8154. www.boone hallfarms.com. Open year-round Mon–Sat 9am–7pm, Sun 10am–6pm.* Located about a mile from the plantation, this large farm market does a brisk business in fresh local produce and preserved goods from Boone Hall. There's an on-site seafood market, a butcher shop, a florist shop and a cafe serving

Boone Hall Farm

Boone Hall is still a working farm, and you can sample its bounty nearly year-round. In spring, come to pick strawberries; in summer there are peaches and tomatoes. October brings pumpkins and hayrides, and in December you can buy fresh-cut Fraser firs. Call or check website for hours and fees.

Oak-lined avenue leading to Boone Hall

PLANTATIONS

Hopsewee Plantation

©Myrtle Beach Area CVB

home-churned ice cream. A wide array of gift items, gourmet foods, wines, cookbooks, baked goods and other groceries are available for purchase.

Boone Hall's Annual Events

- Oyster Festival *Jan*
- Strawberry Festival *Apr*
- Piggly Wiggly BBQ Championship & Bluegrass Festival *Labor Day Weekend*
- Scottish Games and Highland Gathering *Sept*
- Southern Living Taste of Charleston *Oct*
- Boone Hall Pumpkin Patch *Oct*
- Boone Hall Fright Nights *Oct*
- Battle of Secessionville *Nov*
- Living History Weekend *Nov*

Fun Fact
In the late 18C, the wealthy class in Charles Towne was so crazy about rice that local cabinetmakers created the "rice bed," carved with rice ears and leaves on its bedposts—a popular style that's still reproduced today.

- Wine under the Oaks *Dec*
- Boone Hall Plantation Christmas *Dec*

Lowcountry Plantations
There are a couple of plantations that lie a bit farther away north of Charleston (within an hour's drive), and you can visit them on your way up to **Myrtle Beach★**.
For descriptions, see The Grand Strand.

Hopsewee Plantation – *494 Hopsewee Rd., Georgetown. 48mi north of Charleston on US-17 North.*
This Lowcountry indigo plantation was the birthplace of a signer of the Declaration of Independence. Today you can have tea and cake there before or after your tour.

Hampton Plantation State Historic Site – *1950 Rutledge Rd., McClellanville. 47.5mi north of Charleston via US-17 North.*
This rice plantation and its lovely grounds belonged to a French Huguenot family in the 18C. Today you can enjoy its peaceful setting amid massive oak trees.

MUST SEE

Carolina Gold

Luckily for the area's early economy, rice was well-suited to the Lowcountry's hot, humid climate. The crop first came to Carolina from Madagascar by way of slaves, who brought the grains and the knowledge of how to plant them. With its golden hull and fine quality, this particular variety of African rice became known as "Carolina Gold." Shipped to markets throughout Europe, rice ruled as South Carolina's most important product up until the Civil War.

Although the colonists' first attempts at growing rice failed, by 1726 the crop was being grown near tidal rivers where fields could be flooded and later drained. It wasn't easy to cultivate rice. Nearly every task associated with rice growing had to be done by hand, from clearing the land to digging the dikes and ditches that would divert river water to the fields, and milling the rice itself.

These tasks, of course, fell to the slaves, who served as the backbone of the plantations. In the mid-18C, slaves were expected to clear 1,200 square feet of land a day and hand-thresh 600 sheaves of rice. Using sticks called "flails," they beat the rice stalks until the grains fell out; then they separated the grains from the shafts by shaking them in large, flat winnowing baskets. Rice was milled by hand using a mortar and pestle to remove the tough outer husk.

For nearly 200 years, the 300-mile coastline from Cape Fear, North Carolina, to the St. Marys River in Georgia, reigned as the "Kingdom of Rice." In the years before the Civil War, South Carolina counted 227 plantations—with a whopping 70,000 acres of land—in cultivation, which produced an average of 11 million pounds of rice a year. Their fortunes assured by the 1840s, rice-plantation owners became gentlemen of leisure, spending much of their time socializing in their fine Charleston townhouses, and managing their estates from afar.

After the Civil War, planters couldn't afford to pay workers to do the back-breaking labor—once performed by slaves—that growing rice required. Without free labor, it was too costly to cultivate rice, so planters turned to other means of support, such as growing cotton and mining phosphate along the rivers.

Certified Carolina Gold plantation rice can be purchased today at Boone Hall Farms Market (see store hours, p59).

©Brigitta L. House/Michelin

BEACHES

Grab your towel and sunscreen and head for the wide expanses of sand that line the coast north and south of Charleston. From residential Isle of Palms to tony Kiawah, Charleston's barrier-island beaches make a great excursion. Whether you spend the day at one of the area's public beach parks or stay longer at an island resort, you're sure to find fun in the sun that the whole family will enjoy.

PUBLIC BEACH PARKS

Beachwalker County Park

Relaxing in Beachwalker Park

©Charleston County Park and Recreation Commission

21mi south of Charleston. 1 Beachwalker Dr., on the southern end of Kiawah Island. From Charleston, take the James Island Connector and turn right on Folly Rd. Go left on Maybank Hwy. (Rte. 700) to Bohicket Rd. Turn left on Bohicket Rd. and follow signs to Kiawah Island. Turn left on Kiawah Island Pkwy. and take the first right on Beachwalker Dr. 843-768-2395. www.ccprc.com. Open May–Labor Day daily 9am–7pm. Sept daily 10am–6pm. Mar–Apr daily 10am–6pm. Oct Mon–Fri 9am–5pm. Closed Nov–Feb. $7/vehicle.

If you want to experience the spectacular beach on **Kiawah Island**★★ *(see The Lowcountry*

Coast), but don't want to rent lodgings at the private resort, spend a day at Beachwalker Park. Located just outside the resort's gates, the county park offers equipment rentals, lifeguards (in summer), dressing areas, outdoor showers, restrooms, and picnic areas with grills. For supplies, there's a convenience store and gas station right on Beachwalker Drive as you turn off Kiawah Island Parkway.

Pier, Isle of Palms

©Janette Siler/Michelin

🏖 Folly Beach County Park

Closed in 2012 due to beach erosion; check website for updates. 12mi south of Charleston. 1010 West Ashley Ave., on the west end of Folly Island. Take the James Island Connector (Rte. 30) to Folly Rd. Turn left on Folly Rd. and continue 8mi until it ends. Turn right at the light at Ashley Ave. and follow it to the end. 843-795-4386. www.ccprc.com. $8/vehicle (no fee Nov–Feb).

Folly Beach Pier

©Charleston Area CVB

The closest sands to Charleston, bohemian Folly Beach caters to hordes of locals and visitors. Rent an umbrella and some chairs and stake out your spot along the 2,500 feet of oceanfront.

The park offers the same amenities as Beachwalker Park, as well as a snack bar and boogie-board rentals in case the kids forgot their own boards. In summer, lifeguards patrol a designated beach area. Extending 1,045ft out into the water, the nearby **Edwin S. Taylor Folly Beach Fishing Pier** invites avid anglers to drop a line and see what's biting *(see Musts for Fun)*. The biggest fish ever caught from the pier was a 100-pound tarpon in 1996.

Touring Tip

Parking is scant at this county park, which draws throngs of sunseekers on nice summer weekends. Plan to come early if you want a good parking space. Beer-drinkers take note: No alcoholic beverages are permitted on any of the county beaches.

Folly or Folly? – The label Folly Beach originally came from the Old English word meaning "dense foliage," which is likely what the early settlers found along the coast

McKevlin's Surf Shop

8 Center St. 843-588-2247. www.mckevlins.com.
One of the oldest surf shops on the East Coast, McKevlin's established in 1965 by local surfer Dennis McKevlin and his eldest son, Ted. Today the shop boasts 3,300 square feet of retail space filled with surfboards, bodyboards, wax, and car racks. Even if you're not a surfer, it's always cool to have a McKevlin's T-shirt.

©McKevlin's Surf Shop

♦ For the latest on where the best waves are breaking, call McKevlin's **Surf Report:** 843-588-2261.

BEACHES

Beach on Isle of Palms

©Rocky Reston/Dreamstime.com

Sea Turtle Season

©Krill Zdorov/Dreamstime.com

Loggerhead sea turtles *(Caretta caretta)* nest along the coast of South Carolina each year from mid-May through October. Females will dig a nest in the sand, where they lay up to 150 ping-pong-ball-size eggs that will incubate for 54 to 60 days. After emerging from their eggs at night, the hatchlings instinctively move away from the shadows and seek the brightest horizon—normally the ocean. Glaring lights of beachfront development confuse the young turtles, who often head in the wrong direction, decreasing their chances of survival.

The **South Carolina Aquarium**★★ *(see Musts for Kids)* sponsors a sea turtle "head start" program to help this threatened species (all species of sea turtles are either endangered or threatened). Each summer, the aquarium acquires a few loggerhead hatchlings from local beaches and raises them in protected conditions for a couple of years before releasing them into the ocean. Several areas, including Kiawah Island and Folly Beach, have organized groups that patrol the beaches and fence off the turtle nests so that beachgoers don't inadvertently destroy them. If you see signs of turtle activity, please be sure not to disturb the nests.

What's So Cool about Loggerhead Sea Turtles?

◆ Loggerheads can live up to 50 years or more.

◆ Female turtles return to lay their eggs on or near the same beach where they hatched.

◆ Adult loggerheads can weigh anywhere from 170 to 500 pounds; their shell, called a carapace, can grow up to 45 inches in length.

◆ Loggerheads are carnivorous; they use their powerful jaws to devour a variety of fish and shellfish.

◆ Loggerhead sea turtles have been officially listed as a threatened species since 1978.

here. Today, though, the tiny beach town with its carefree attitude identifies more with the modern definition of the word.

Isle of Palms County Park

12mi northeast of Charleston. 1–14th Aves., Isle of Palms (between Palm Blvd. & Ocean Blvd.). Take US-17 North to the Isle of Palms Connector (Rte. 517). When the connector ends at Palm Blvd., go straight through the light and follow signs. 843-886-3863. www.ccprc.com. Open May–Labor Day daily 9am–7pm. Mar–Apr & Sept–Oct daily 10am–6pm. Nov–Feb daily 10am–5pm. $8/ vehicle (no fee Nov–Feb).

Just a 25-minute drive north of downtown Charleston, the six-mile-long **Isle of Palms** makes a great escape from the city's often-crowded urban streets. This is a real beach community, with a large year-round population. Besides lifeguards (in summer) and all the other amenities found at Folly Beach and Beachwalker Park, Isle of Palms County Park has a children's play area and a sand volleyball court. Directly behind the beach you'll find a recently spruced-up commercial strip featuring metered parking, shops, beachfront bars *(see p 113),* and an outpost of Ben and Jerry's ice cream *(closed in winter).* The pier here is not open to the public.

♦ **Best Surfing** – The coast from the pier up to 30th Street.

BEACH RESORTS

The following are brief descriptions of three resort areas. For fuller descriptions, see The Grand Strand and The Lowcountry Coast.

Beach Rentals

Prices for rentals at all three county beach parks: 1 chair, $10/day; 1 umbrella $10/day; or save a few bucks by renting 2 chairs and 1 umbrella for $25/day. If you come after 4pm, when the crowds start to leave, rental fees drop to $5 for one chair or one umbrella.

Umbrellas and rental chairs on the beach

©South Carolina Department of Parks, Recreation & Tourism, DiscoverSouthCarolina.com

BEACHES

Shelling on the Coast

Despite the fact that Blackbeard once prowled South Carolina's shore, the buried treasure you're most likely to find on these beaches is of the mollusk variety. Hunting for seashells can provide hours of fun for both kids and their parents. The wealth of seashells you might uncover at low tide—the best time to hunt for shells—includes fuzzy gray sand dollars, striped lightning whelks, snail-like baby's ears, colorful calico scallops, slender augers, and Atlantic clams. Remember one rule of thumb: Never take shells with live creatures in them; you don't want to disturb some critter's home!

©Myrtle Beach Area Chamber of Commerce

The Grand Strand★★

Myrtle Beach is 98mi north of Charleston via US-17.

The excitement of **Myrtle Beach★** and the quieter Grand Strand resort areas of Litchfield Beach and Pawleys Island are less than a two-hour drive north of Charleston.

Kiawah Island★★

21mi south of Charleston via US-17. See The Lowcountry Coast.

A luxurious resort with amenities galore tucks into the marshland and maritime forest on this private island. Five championship golf courses include the famed Ocean Course. From a family vacation to a romantic couples' getaway at the sumptuous Sanctuary hotel, you'll find your niche on Kiawah.

Wild Dunes★

15mi north of Charleston on Isle of Palms. See The Lowcountry Coast.

This private beach resort occupies the northern tip of Isle of Palms. Golfers and tennis players come for the courses and clay courts, while families favor the beach. Lodgings include houses, condos and an oceanfront hotel.

Beach on Kiawah Island

© Jason Tench/Dreamstime.com

MUST SEE

PARKS AND GARDENS

With its semi-tropical climate, Charleston flowers year-round with a splashy variety of blooms from camellias and winter jessamine *(Jan–Feb)*, **azaleas and magnolias** *(Apr–May)* **to roses and crepe myrtles** *(Jun–Aug).* **And since it's warm out more months than not here, you can enjoy the city's parks and gardens in every season.**

Peninsula Parks

Waterfront Park★

Cumberland St. to Tradd St. 843-724-7327. www.charlestoncity.info.

Set along Charleston Harbor, in the historic district, this 8-acre linear park occupies the space once filled by the old port's wharves. A fanciful **pineapple fountain** marks its center. In warm weather (which is most of the year in Charleston) kids love to run through the **circular fountain** by the pier (at the end of Vendue Range). Joggers and walkers favor the paved walkway that hugs the waterfront, and the park's spacious green lawns make a great place for a picnic *(see Musts for Fun)*. On the inland side of the park, small landscaped "garden rooms" provide peaceful nooks for outdoor reading.

Pineapple fountain, Waterfront Park

©ExploreCharleston.com

Pier – *At the end of Vendue Range.* This pleasant 400-foot pier jutting out into the harbor provides picnic tables and wooden swings for taking in the water views. Bring

Waterfront Park

©Brigitta L. House/Michelin

Glorious Gardens

843-722-3405. www.historiccharleston.org. $45. Held every Thursday during the annual Festival of Houses and Gardens *(mid-Mar–mid-Apr; see p 85)*, Glorious Gardens self-guided walking tours take you inside the gates of as many as 8 to 10 private gardens in the historic district during the city's peak blooming season. Here you'll see plots bright with azaleas, dogwoods, magnolias, jasmine, tea olives and other spring blossoms; after the tour, there's a reception in the garden of the Nathaniel Russell House *(51 Meeting St.; see Historic District)*.

your rod and reel to see what's biting.

White Point Gardens★

Along the Battery, at the intersection of East Bay St. & Murray Blvd. 843-724-7327. www.charlestoncity.info.

Named for the gleaming white oyster beds that the first settlers found on this site in 1670, White Point occupies the southern tip of Charleston's peninsula. It was here that the settlers relocated their fledgling town in 1680.

This strategic point at the junction of the Ashley and Cooper rivers was used to defend the city as far back as the early 1700s, when the original walls were built around the new town. Established as a public park in 1837, White Point was again used as a gun battery during the Civil War. A number of Confederate cannons still stand in the park as reminders of less peaceful times. Monuments here honor heroes from the Revolutionary War and the Civil War, including the crew of the *H.L. Hunley (see Historic Sites)*. The gracious four-block-long park that you see today was laid out in 1906 by John Charles Olmsted (stepson of renowned landscape architect Frederick Law Olmsted, whose credits include New York's Central Park). Also referred to simply as The Battery *(see Historic District)*, White Point Gardens makes a wonderful spot for strolling, picnicking *(see Musts for Fun)* or just relaxing amid its palmettos and moss-draped live

White Point Gardens

©Brigitta L. House/Michelin

White Point Gallows

In its early days, Charles Towne was plagued by pirates, including the notorious Edward Teach, aka "Blackbeard," who captured several ships in Charleston Harbor in 1718. But perhaps Charleston's most famous rogue was Stede Bonnet, the well-educated son of a wealthy Barbadian family who turned to piracy after serving as a major in the Barbados army. Whether Bonnet became a pirate to escape his wife's incessant nagging, as legend has it, or whether his whim "proceeded from a disorder of his mind," as his cronies believed, remains anyone's guess.

Called "the gentleman pirate" for his cultured manner, Bonnet took part in Blackbeard's siege of Charleston Harbor. In 1718 Bonnet was captured on the Cape Fear River in North Carolina and brought back to Charleston to stand trial for his crimes. Despite his gentlemanly behavior, Bonnet was sentenced to hang in White Point Gardens—along with 49 other pirates who met the same fate later that year (Bonnet's letter pleading for his life is on display in the Old Provost Dungeon; *see Historic Sites*). A plaque in the park commemorates Bonnet and the other pirates who met their end in White Point Gardens.

oak trees. Of course, the expansive view out to the horizon is not bad, either. You can even see Fort Sumter in the distance (look for its flagpole).

Hampton Park

Entrance on Cleveland St., off Rutledge Ave. 843-724-7327. www.charlestonparksconservancy.org.

Just outside the Citadel's gates and bounded by Mary Murray Drive, Hampton Park embraces 60 acres of lovely recreational space, including a rose garden, a concert bandstand, and trails for walking, biking or jogging. There's

Statue in Hampton Park
©Doug Rogers/Michelin

Kids Run

Drawing 45,000 participants, one of Charleston's biggest athletic events is the 10K Cooper River Bridge Run, held every April. For years, the event's sponsors have hosted a Kids Run the day before the adult race. In 2004, the Kids Run moved to Hampton Park and turned into a whole afternoon of fun. Kids of all ages are invited to participate; the festivities start with a 25-yard dash for toddlers and go up to a 1-mile run for ages 8 to 13. Even if your little ones don't want to run, they can still climb the rock wall, visit the petting zoo and play on the jump castle and super slide. *Registration is required for the race: $8 in advance ($10 at event); 843-792-0345; www.bridgerun.com.*

Aerial view of Middleton Place gardens

© Middleton Place, Charleston, South Carolina

a large lake with a fountain that shoots water high into the air. In spring azaleas and camellias are in bloom here. Visitors can enjoy the picnic tables, large shade trees, a well-equipped playground and ball fields too.

West Ashley Gardens

Middleton Place Gardens★★★

4300 Ashley River Rd. 843-556-6020. www.middletonplace.org. Open year-round daily 9am–5pm. Closed Dec 25. General admission (gardens & grounds) $25 adults, $10 children (free for children under age 6). See Plantations.

America owes its oldest landscaped gardens to moneyed plantation owner Henry Middleton, who laid them out in classic European style in 1741. The main sight line slopes down from the entrance gates over terraces above the twin "butterfly" lakes (shaped like two butterfly wings) to the Ashley River just beyond. More than 100 slaves spent 10 years digging ornamental canals, planting shrubs and forming the land to Middleton's

elaborate plan. In keeping with 18C ideals of a garden, his plan called for symmetrical "galleries" walled in by greenery, and views reaching down to the river across wide, grassy lawns.

Opened to the public in the 1920s, Middleton's masterpiece has been added to over the years; new plantings now color the original

Camellia Walks at Middleton Place

From February to March, Middleton Place sponsors special guided walks that spotlight its prized collection of lovely camellias. Of the hundreds of varieties planted here, the oldest camellia dates back to 1786. Tours last 1½ hours and are held on selected days *(call or check website for the schedule)* beginning at 11am. Reservations are required.

©Brigitta L. House/Michelin

MUST SEE

plan, so that the gardens bloom 12 months of the year.

Magnolia Plantation★★

3550 Ashley River Rd. 843-571-1266. www.magnoliaplantation.com. Open Mar–Oct daily 8am–5:30pm. Rest of the year daily 8am–4:30pm. $15 adults, $10 children (ages 6–12). See Plantations.

Azaleas rule. At least they do at Magnolia's 50 acres of gardens from mid-March through April, when some 250 different varieties of azaleas paint the canal banks in vibrant pink, white and purple. There are also the twisting wisteria vines dripping with clusters of lavender flowers, delicate yellow forsythia, fragrant honeysuckle and pink and white dogwoods—don't forget your camera!

In summer you'll find magnolias along with lilies and wildflowers. In fall and winter some 900 types of camellias flower; more than 150 of them were developed here on the plantation.

Garden Highlights

After Reverend John Grimke Drayton inherited Magnolia

Anhinga in Magnolia Plantation

©Brigitta L. House/Michelin

Bird Walk

Birders, take note: every Sunday morning at 8:30am, Magnolia Plantation sponsors a guided bird walk to see some of the 254 species that have been spotted here. You might observe great blue herons, coots, anhingas, egrets, gallinules and bald eagles during the 2.5-hour tour. Ask at the Admissions Gate for the walk's starting point. Tickets are $17 and include basic admission to the garden and grounds.

Azaleas, Magnolia Plantation

©Magnolia Plantation

Plantation in 1820, he developed the existing gardens, enhancing the natural landscape, rather than creating a formal garden such as the one at Middleton Place. He is credited with introducing the first *Azalea Indica* to America in the mid-19C.

Long White Bridge – Reverend Drayton built this graceful arched garden landmark in the 1840s to span a natural river marsh.

Biblical Garden – What plants might have grown in the Garden of Eden? You'll find some of the answers in this educational plot.

Barbados Tropical Garden – Since the original owner of the plantation hailed from Barbados, it's only fitting that the plantation displays some of that island's flora.

Maze – Kids—and adults—will love getting lost in this labyrinth, modeled on the boxwood maze that King Henry VIII designed for his country estate in the 16C. Instead of using the boxwood, though, this maze is fashioned from camellias and hollies. See if you can find your way out!

Audubon Swamp Garden★

At Magnolia Gardens, 3550 Ashley River Rd. 843-571-1266. www.magnoliaplantation.com. Open year-round daily 8am– 5:30pm. $8 adults & children (ages 6–12). Children under 6 are admitted free.

Covering an eerie 60 acres of blackwater cypress and tupelo swamp, this area was added to Magnolia Plantation in the 1980s. It takes its name from early-19C naturalist John James Audubon, who visited Magnolia Plantation to study waterbirds during one of his many trips to Charleston. Allow at least an hour to wander the boardwalks and bridges through the swamp and give yourself ample time to take in the

Swamp Thing

The murky water of Audubon Swamp Garden made a fitting setting for the 1982 horror flick, *The Swamp Thing*, starring Louis Jourdan and Adrienne Barbeau.

Alligator, Audubon Swamp Garden

©Magnolia Plantation

Be sure to bring bug spray if you're visiting the gardens in warm weather—especially in summer. As in any swampy setting, the mosquitoes can be pretty pesky.

Rollerblading in James Island County Park

©Charleston County Park and Recreation Commission

colors and textures of the place, such as brilliant green duckweed that makes the water appear solid, knobby black silhouettes of cypress knees, lacy ferns and bright lilies. Keep your eye out for wildlife along the way. White ibis, blue-winged teals, great blue herons and snowy egrets are just a tiny sampling of the more than 200 types of birds that have been seen at the swamp gardens. Otters, turtles and, of course, alligators are also ever-present denizens here.

Beach and County Parks

Whether you're beaching it or not, try one of these area county parks, usually open to the public daily year-round *(www.ccprc.com)*.

Beachwalker County Park –

1 Beachwalker Dr., Kiawah Island. This county park on otherwise private Kiawah Island is open March through October. *See Beaches.*

Folly Beach County Park –

1010 West Ashley Ave., at the south end of Folly Rd. Charleston's beach packs in the crowds on summer weekends. *See Beaches.*

Isle of Palms County Park –

1-14th Aves., Isle of Palms. A 25-minute drive north of Charleston brings you to this wide public beach. *See Beaches.*

James Island County Park –

871 Riverland Dr., on James Island. OK, this one's not a beach, but it's still lots of fun for the whole family. *See Musts for Kids.*

Angel Oak

It's rare to find a tree that's outlived logging, hurricanes and earthquakes, but this live oak *(Quercus virginiana)* has done just that. Estimated to be 1,400 years old, the 65-foot-high Angel Oak spreads its branches 160 feet around. It's worth a drive—especially if you're headed to Kiawah Island *(see The Lowcountry Coast)*—to see this ancient oak. Pack a picnic when you come; even on the hottest summer day, Angel Oak shades an area of 17,000 square feet. *3688 Angel Oak Rd., Johns Island. See map of Charleston Urban Area, p 48. From Charleston, take the James Island connector to Folly Rd. and turn right; turn left on Maybank Hwy./Rte. 700 and take it to Bohicket Rd. (follow signs for Kiawah Island). Turn left on Bohicket Rd. and follow signs to Angel Oak (on the right). www.angeloaktree.org.*

PARKS AND GARDENS

MUSEUMS

Charleston may not harbor a lot of museums, but the handful it does have are well worth a look. Take a sailor's-eye view of maritime history at Patriots Point; peek at Lowcountry artistic traditions at the Gibbes Museum; and travel back through time at the Charleston Museum.

USS Yorktown, Patriots Point Naval & Maritime Museum

©Patriots Point Naval & Maritime Museum

Patriots Point Naval & Maritime Museum★★

3mi north of Charleston in Mt. Pleasant. Take US-17 North across the bridge and follow signs for Rte. 703. Take the first right on Patriots Point Rd. 843-884-2727. www.patriotspoint.org. Open year-round daily 9am–6:30pm. Closed Dec 25. $18 adults, $11 children (ages 6–11). Free for children under age 6. Parking $5.

You may have wondered what that huge gray shape is across the harbor from Charleston. It's the World War II aircraft carrier the **USS Yorktown★★**, the centerpiece of Patriots Point. Built to honor the men and women who have served in the US Navy in the 20C, Patriots Point features four historic vessels, a mock-up of a US Navy base camp in Vietnam, the Medal of Honor Museum and the Cold War Submarine Memorial *(across the*

parking lot on Charleston Harbor). Dubbed the "Fighting Lady," the *Yorktown* was commissioned in Newport News, Virginia, in 1943. During World War II, she carried a crew of 380 officers and 3,038 enlisted men, along with 90 aircraft on board.

After the war she served in Vietnam, and later recovered the astronauts from *Apollo 8* when they returned from their moon

Inside the Pilot Ready Room

©Patriots Point Naval & Maritime Museum

Allow at least two hours—although you could easily spend longer—to explore the *Yorktown* and the other ships. Scrambling up and down through the decks of the *Yorktown* can be tricky; access is by ladder-like stairways, and requires a certain amount of agility. Patriots Point is one of the two places that you can catch a boat to **Fort Sumter★★★**; the other is at Aquarium Wharf *(see Historic Sites)*. For schedules, call 843-884-2727.

orbit in 1968. The *Yorktown* was decommissioned in 1970; the ship was towed from New Jersey to Charleston five years later.

You're free to roam this vast, 888-foot-long floating museum from engine room to bridge, following any of six self-guided tours that take you through five lower decks and seven levels above the hangar bay.

In all you'll find 26 naval aircraft on board, some in the hangar bay, others up on the flight deck. Two additional World War II ships are berthed at Patriots Point:

♦ **USS Clamagore** World War II submarine
♦ **USS Laffey** DD724 Destroyer

Charleston Museum★

360 Meeting St. 843-722-2996. www.charlestonmuseum.org. Open year-round Mon–Sat 9am–5pm, Sun 1pm–5pm. Closed major holidays. $10 adults, $5 children (ages 3-12). Combination tickets are available for the museum and the Heyward-Washington and Joseph Manigault house (see Historic District).

Located across the street from the Visitor Center, the Charleston Museum is a good place to begin your tour of the city. Exhibits in this contemporary brick structure cover Charleston and the Lowcountry's social and natural history from pre-settlement days to the present. The scope of the museum's collection ranges from a prehistoric crocodile skeleton to a scale model of a Civil War-era submarine.

What's What in the Museum?

South Carolina Lowcountry – The museum's largest permanent exhibit begins with the area's geology and earliest native inhabitants. It tells the story of Charleston from its first settlers, through the Revolution and the city's plantation heyday, to the Civil War and Reconstruction, and finally to the 20C. Objects, including Revolutionary War swords, sweetgrass baskets used to process rice, and Victorian furnishings, illustrate each period in the city's long history.

Charleston Museum for Kids

History isn't always boring; kids of all ages will be able to find something of interest here. Every Wednesday in June and July at 3:30pm *(free with admission)*, guided Kids Tours focus on a particular artifact in the museum's collection, such as the Egyptian mummy or the dinosaur skeleton. The hands-on Kids Story exhibit brings Lowcountry history to life, while Lowcountry Stories highlight a multimedia story-telling station.

Examples from Silver Collection Charleston Museum

©Courtesy of The Charleston Museum, Charleston, SC

The Early Days – An Egyptian mummy and taxidermed polar bear may not have much connection to the Lowcountry, but they are among the artifacts from the original museum, which was located in Thompson Auditorium nearby. Founded in 1773, the old museum provided a "window on the world" with its casts of ancient Roman statues, specimens, and skeletons of prehistoric animals.

Charleston Silver – The museum showcases fine holdings of 18C and 19C silver made in Charleston. George Washington's christening cup is one of the collection's treasures.

Gibbes Museum of Art★

135 Meeting St. 843-722-2706. www.gibbesmuseum.org. Open year-round Tue–Sat 10am–5pm, Sun 1pm–5pm. Closed Mon & major holidays. $9.

American art with a "Charleston perspective"—that's what you'll find at the Gibbes. Most of the more than 15,000 objects in the museum, which opened in 1905, showcase works that have some connection to the Lowcountry, whether they were created in Charleston, done by local artists, collected by the city's residents, or simply portray life in the Charleston area. The permanent collection

The Charleston Renaissance

Charleston's renaissance was a cultural one. In the mid-1920s, Charleston's antebellum mansions were crumbling, its economy depressed. Enter a group of local artists and writers, who sought to bring attention to the city's rich cultural heritage. Writer DuBose Heyward—who penned the 1925 book *Porgy*, on which composer George Gershwin based his folk opera *Porgy and Bess* in 1935; and Charleston painter Elizabeth O'Neill Verner, along with others, all interpreted the Lowcountry folkways in their art. Their music, books and canvases created images of daily life of Charleston and the nearby plantations for the world to see. The cultural renewal they launched, later known as the Charleston Renaissance, emphasized American values and realism; the sense of civic pride it fostered would eventually fuel Charleston's historic-preservation movement *(see p 34)*.

occupies the first floor; most of the gallery space on the second floor contains changing exhibits.

Art in the South—The Charleston Perspective – This collection of more than 500 paintings focuses on 18C, 19C and 20C American art by the likes of Benjamin West, Gilbert Stuart, Thomas Sully, and Henrietta Johnston, who's hailed as America's first professional female artist. Included in this group of paintings are works by Charleston Renaissance artists Elizabeth O'Neill Verner, Alice Ravenel Huger Smith and Anna Heyward Taylor.

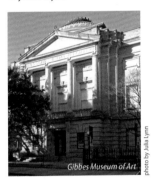

Gibbes Museum of Art

photo by Julia Lynn

Rice Plantation Series – In 1937 artist Alice Ravenel Huger Smith (1876–1958) donated 30 original watercolors to the museum; these paintings now make up one of the museum's most significant collections.

Miniature Portrait Collection – The museum's 600 examples of tiny paintings, conceived as tokens of affection, encompass works by English, French and American artists. They span the years from the 18C through the early 20C.

Children's Museum of the Lowcountry

25 Ann St. See Musts for Kids.

The Citadel Museum

On The Citadel campus.
See Historic Sites.

Confederate Museum

188 Meeting St., at the corner of Market St. 843-723-1541. Open year-round Tue–Sat 11am–3:30pm. Closed Sun, Mon & major holidays. $5.

Established by the Daughters of the Confederacy in 1898, this collection in Market Hall *(second floor; see Historic District)* contains an important group of artifacts and archives of documents from the Civil War, including uniforms, weapons, flags and historic photographs.

American Military Museum

2070 Sam Rittenberg Blvd. 843-577-7000. www.american militarymuseum.org. Open year-round Mon–Sat 10am–6pm, Sun 1pm–5pm. Closed Thanksgiving Day & Dec 25. $9 ($7 for veterans).

Located in the Citadel Mall, the museum is filled with uniforms, weaponry, medals, and personal artifacts belonging to soldiers from all branches of the US military service. Exhibits are arranged chronologically beginning with the present—the Iraq conflict—and going back to the Revolutionary War. There's even a case full of miniature soldiers that will appeal to the young at heart.

MUSEUMS

FOR FUN

Despite its mannerly exterior, Charleston isn't above laughing at itself. In fact, the Holy City likes to let its hair down once in a while for some good old-fashioned fun. Here are some suggestions for quintessentially Charleston things to do.

Carriage Tour

©ExploreCharleston.com

EXPLORE CHARLESTON

🐎 Carriage Tours

It would be a shame to visit Charleston and not clip-clop around the historic district in one of the handsome horse- or mule-drawn carriages that share the city's downtown streets with more modern vehicles. The carriage rides are a leisurely way to get an eye-level overview of the historic district. Along the way, your driver/guide will no doubt provide a witty—though not always historically accurate—narration of local history and lore.

There are a number of different companies that provide carriage tours. Choose the one that appeals to you by checking out the lineup along Anson and North Market streets, near the Old City Market. Tours generally last one hour and cost an average of $22 for adults and $14 for children.

Here are some of the favorites:

- **Classic Carriage Tours** – *10 Guignard St. 843-853-3747. www.classiccarriage.com.*
- **Old South Carriage Company** – *14 Anson St. 843-723-9712. www.oldsouthcarriagetours.com.*
- **Palmetto Carriage Tours** – *8 Guignard St. 843-723-8145. www.palmettocarriage.com.*

Drinks with a View

Charleston may not have many high-rise buildings, but that doesn't mean there's no place for panoramic views. Here are a couple of rooftops where the cognoscenti go for cocktails:

🍸 Pavilion Bar –

Top floor of the Market Pavilion Hotel, 225 East Bay St., at the corner of Market St. 843-723-0500. www.marketpavilion.com. Open Sun–Thu 11:30am–midnight, Fri & Sat 11:30am–2am.

MUST DO

The Rooftop, Vendue Inn

©Vendue Inn

The historic district's rooftops and the harbor stretch out below you as you relax at this chic Charleston hot spot. Grab a table or a seat at the bar and order a cocktail, or perhaps nibble an appetizer from the light-fare menu. Go before dinner to watch the sunset and sip an aperitif, or stop by later for a brandy and dessert.

Rooftop Bar and Restaurant – *Top floor of the Vendue Inn, 19 Vendue Range, off East Bay St. 843-577-7970. www.vendueinn.com. Open daily 11:30am–midnight.* Charleston's original rooftop bar offers great views along with appetizers. You can listen to live music here nightly (6:30pm–9:30pm).

Ghostly Charleston

Face it, a city as old as Charleston is bound to have its share of ghosts. And Charleston does, if you believe the local lore. You can meet—hopefully not face to face—some of the city's favorite spirits on one of the following ghost tours. Leave the little ones at home and take to Charleston's venerable streets and cemeteries with a guide after dark for an eerie adventure. You'll be scared you did!

The 90-minute walking tours listed on the next page all require reservations (call for schedule). Due to the potentially frightening nature of the tours, children under age 7 are not permitted.

Sweet Tea in the South

The universal drink among Southerners, iced tea is traditionally made from brewed tea with lots of sugar. When you ask for iced tea in a restaurant in the South, you will automatically be served "sweet tea"—as it's called in the South—unless you specify "unsweetened."

French botanist André Michaux, a friend of Arthur Middleton, brought the first tea plants to the US in the 1700s. Tea was originally planted in the Charleston area at what is now Middleton Place *(see Plantations)*, and the crop still grows in the region today. For a close-up view, visit the **Charleston Tea Plantation** on Wadmalaw Island *(843-559-0383; ww.charlestonteaplantation.com).*

FOR FUN

Haunted Jail Tour

©Bulldog Tours

The Ghosts of Charleston – *Tours depart from Waterfront Park, at the end of Vendue Range, daily at 5pm, 7pm & 9:30pm. 843-723-1670. www.tourcharleston.com. Tours daily at 5pm, 7:30pm & 9:30pm. $18 adults, $12 children (ages 7–14).* Aside from a spooky walk through the historic district, this company offers another tour (Ghosts II) that takes in the edges of town (departs from Marion Square).

The Ghosts & Legends of Charleston – *Tours depart from 58½ Broad St. nightly 5:30pm, 7:30pm & 9:30pm (except Jan 1 & Dec 25). 843-534-7302. www.charlestonwalks. com. $14.50 adults, $9 children (ages 7-14).* You'll walk a little over a mile on this tour, perhaps shaking in

your boots at some points.

Ghost and Dungeon Walking Tour – *Tours depart from 40 N. Market St., nightly 7pm & 9pm. 843-722-8687. www.bulldogtours.com. $18 adults, $10 children (ages 7-12).* The tour includes a walk through Charleston's Provost Dungeon *(see Historic District).*

Harbor Cruises

Cruising the rivers around the Charleston peninsula makes a great family excursion on a pretty day. Whether you do a harbor tour, a dinner cruise or a nature excursion, being out on the water will give you a new perspective of the city. Here are a few places to start; you can get a complete listing of harbor tours at the Visitor Center at 375

The Lady in White

If you happen to be wandering around the eerie tree-shrouded graveyard of Charleston's Unitarian Church *(4 Archdale St.)* at night, keep an eye out for the city's most frequently seen ghost, known as the "Lady in White." According to Julian T. Buxton, author of *The Ghosts of Charleston,* the spirit of Mary Bloomfield White (she died in 1907) haunts the churchyard here searching for her husband, whose plot next to hers lies empty. Her spouse died on the same date as Mary did, 500 miles away, in Baltimore, Maryland. To this day, no one knows the location of his grave. For the rest of the story, check out Buxton's book or take the Ghosts of Charleston tour *(above)* given by Tour Charleston.

Gullah Tours

Tours depart from the bus shed at 43 John St. (across from the Charleston Visitor Center) year-round Mon–Fri 11am & 1pm, Sat 11am, 1pm & 3pm. $18 adults, $12 children. 843-763-7551 (reservations requested). www.gullahtours.com.

Hop aboard an air-conditioned bus for an introduction to Charleston's rich African-American heritage, including the intriguing Gullah culture *(see page 140)*. See Catfish Row, the setting of *Porgy and Bess*; meet sweetgrass basketmakers; view the many ornate iron gates crafted by Philip Simmons; and learn how the Underground Railroad operated in Charleston. You'll do all this and more on the two-hour excursion guided by local lecturer and resident Alphonso Brown.

Meeting Street. Call for schedules (they vary seasonally) before you go.

SpiritLine – *843-722-2628 or 800-789-3678. www.spiritlinecruises.com. Harbor tour Mar–Nov. $17 adults, $10 children (ages 6-11).*
SpiritLine's 90-minute narrated harbor tours depart from Aquarium Wharf and Patriots Point. Three-hour dinner cruises depart from Patriots Point. The company also provides boat transport to **Fort Sumter★★★** *(see Historic Sites).*

Dolphin Discovery Sunset Cruises – *Depart from Isle of Palms Marina (41st Ave., next to the General Store) May–Aug Wed, Fri & Sun 5:30pm. Rest of the year Sun & Wed, call for times. 843-886-5000. www.nature-*

tours.com. $34 adults, $24 children (ages 12 & under).
On this 2.5-hour naturalist-led excursion, you're likely to see bottlenose dolphins and maybe even local sea turtles. A stop at undeveloped Capers Island is included.

Sandlapper Nature Tours – *Tours depart from the Maritime Center (Wharfside St., adjacent to the South Carolina Aquarium). Call or check website for schedules. 843-849-8687. www.sandlappertours. com. $30 adults; $17 children (under age 12).* This naturalist-led tour will appeal to both kids and nature lovers, since it includes a stop at a barrier-island beach to hunt for shells. Tide willing, the boat may

Sandlapper Water Tours

©Sandlapper Water Tours

FOR FUN

Muscadine grapes at Irvin House Vineyards

©Irvin House Vineyards

wander down a salt-marsh creek to spot water birds and dolphins.

Irvin House Vineyards

6775 Bear's Bluff Rd., Wadmalaw Island. 25mi south of Charleston via Maybank Hwy./Rte. 700. 843-559-6867. www.charlestonwine.com. Open for tastings Thu–Sat 10am–5pm. Free tours Sat at 2pm.

South Carolina isn't exactly known for its wine production, but here's a surprise: Muscadine grapes, native to the southeast, thrive in the Lowcountry's hot, humid climate. And in the right hands, they make some decent wine. See for yourself at 48-acre Irvin House Vineyards, Charleston's only vineyard, set amid live oaks and flower gardens on Wadmalaw Island *(a 30-minute drive south of downtown)*. Five varieties (three reds, two whites), all priced at $10 a bottle at the winery, range in character from the dry Mullet Hall Red to the crisp, sweet white called Magnolia. The lovely labels, done by local artists, alone are worth the price.

🌿 Savor the Flavors

Savor the Flavors of Charleston tour departs from 40 Market St., Mon & Sat 9:30am & 2pm. Reservations required. 843-722-8687 or 800-918-0701. www.culinarytours ofcharleston.com. $42/person.

Irvin House Vineyards

©Irvin House Vineyards

MUST DO

Who knew history could be so delicious? At least it is during this 2.5-hour culinary walking tour called "Savor the Flavor," led by guides that know their Charleston history—especially as it relates to regional foodways.

During the tour, you'll make three stops that spotlight local food artisans or food products. Count on sipping and sampling some of the Lowcountry's most iconic foods, such as sweet tea, stone-ground grits, benne wafers and Southern pralines. In season, you'll stop at the Saturday farmers' market *(see Shopping)*, to ogle the luscious produce from local farmers. Wherever you stop, you're sure to come away with a first-hand taste

Touring Tip

The 2.5-hour walking food tour covers a distance of approximately 2 miles, so be sure to wear comfortable walking shoes. Wear a hat and sunscreen in the summer—Charleston's heat and humidity can be oppressive.

of Charleston's food heritage. Serious foodies will want to take the **Kitchen Tour**, which takes groups behind the scenes in some of the best restaurant kitchens in the city. Meet some of Charleston's acclaimed chefs and get some insight into how they whip up all those stellar meals.

Lowcountry Cuisine

Named for the marshy prairies that line the low-lying South Carolina Coast north and south of Charleston, the Lowcountry is remarkable for its cuisine as well as its geography. Traditional Lowcountry cooking, like any regional cuisine, evolved using the ingredients at hand.

Flavored by rice and okra that the slaves brought from West Africa; spices that came with settlers from the West Indies; grits ground from local corn; and plentiful shrimp, crab and oysters—the trilogy of shellfish caught off the city's coast—Charleston's sophisticated fare makes for some mighty good eating.

©Kiawah Island Golf Resort

You'll find all these foods featured prominently on Charleston's restaurant menus. Here are a few must-try dishes while you're in town:

Shrimp and grits – Everyone seems to have his or her own version of this local staple, a combination of local shrimp, fired up with spicy tasso ham and ladled over creamy grits.

She-crab soup – Milk-based she-crab soup, a Charleston invention, is more often than not served spiked with sherry.

Benne seed wafers – Benne is the term African slaves used for sesame seeds, which they brought to the area from West Africa in the 17C. You'll find the sweet wafers sold all over the city; they make great souvenirs for your foodie friends.

FOR FUN

83

Festival Fun

Beginning in January with the Oyster Festival and ending in December with holiday happenings, Charleston's festivals offer a year-round roster of fun for all ages.

Lowcountry Oyster Festival – *Boone Hall Plantation, Long Point Rd., off US-17 in Mt. Pleasant. 843-577-4030. www.charleston restaurantassociation.com. $20 ($15 in advance; children under age 10 free).* Native Americans introduced settlers to roasted oysters in the 17C, and today the Lowcountry oyster roast is a time-honored tradition. The self-proclaimed "world's largest oyster festival" takes place each year in late January or early February (depending on the schedule of the Super Bowl) in Mt. Pleasant. When they say "large," they're not kidding: 65,000 pounds—that's two tractor-trailer loads—of select oysters have been trucked to the grounds of Boone Hall Plantation (*see Plantations*) in the past. Along with oysters at the day-long fête, there are prizes for the best oyster recipe, the most oysters shucked and the most oysters eaten in the shortest time. Kids get awards for the best oyster costume.

Charleston Wine + Food Festival – *Marion Square. 843-727-9998. www.charlestonwineandfood. com. Events priced from $25 up to $1,000.* Take a generous handful of acclaimed Charleston chefs, add a pinch of national vintners, and stir in a dash of top chefs from across the US, and you have a gourmet recipe for a good time. Held the first weekend of March each year and staged in Marion Square, this festival is a foodie's fantasy. Four days of fun begin on Thursday night with the opening event, the **Salute to Charleston's Chefs**. This party, devoted to local talent, features food and wine stations arranged inside a large tent. You'll be entertained by live music as you sample and sip the night away. To taste the combined skills of Charleston chefs who team up with top chefs from across the US, make reservations for one of the **Perfectly Paired Dinners**. on Friday night. Held at different Charleston restaurants, these dinners offer attendees an opportunity to select where they wish to dine based on who's behind the stoves.

For an all-star experience, go for broke (this is the most expensive event by far) and sign up for **Food + Wine with a View**. Held in a private penthouse, this no-holds-barred dinner is prepared by celebrity chefs (who in past years have included Tom Colicchio, Richard Reddington, Mark Vetri and Michael Tusk) and acclaimed vintners. During the day, you can watch cooking demonstrations, try different dishes, and introduce yourself to a host of wines in the **Culinary Village** tents. There are also wine and beer seminars, cookbook signings, luncheons and much more.

Festivities wind up deliciously on Sunday with the **Lowcountry Gospel Brunch** in the morning, and **BBQ, Blues + Brew** in the afternoon. Festival events sell out early, so don't wait to purchase your tickets (they go on sale in September).

Broad Street Tour, Festival of Houses and Gardens

©Leigh Handal, Historic Charleston Foundation

concurrently with the big event, and spotlights local and regional talent.

Patriots Point 4th of July Blast – *Patriots Point, off US-17 in Mt. Pleasant. 843-884-2727. www.patriotspoint.org. Free admission. $5 parking.* What could be more patriotic than fireworks launched from the deck of the World War II aircraft carrier USS *Yorktown*? Come see for yourself as Charleston celebrates the 4th of July at Patriots Point. Enjoy live bands, food, crafts, and the Kidz Zone play area from 5pm until 10:30pm. The main event, the fireworks, starts just after 9pm.

Holiday Parade of Boats – *Charleston Harbor. 843-724-7305. www.charlestonarts.org.* Stake out your place early at one of the official designated viewing sites *(Waterfront Park; the USS Yorktown, at Patriots Point in Mt. Pleasant; and along the Battery)* for this

Festival of Houses and Gardens – *Historic District. 843-722-3405. www.historiccharleston.org. $45.* Here's your opportunity to peek inside some of Charleston's elegant historic private homes. Every spring *(mid-Mar–mid-Apr)*, a host of residents open their doors to the public. During this month-long festival, which celebrated its 65th year in 2012, you can choose among tours (organized by street) that take in private homes in 11 different neighborhoods. Spring is one of Charleston's high seasons, so make reservations for this popular event well in advance.

Spoleto★★ – *Various locations around the city. 843-579-3100. www. spoletousa.org. See Performing Arts.* Playing up international performing arts, this 17-day festival beginning in late May was founded in 1977 by Maestro Gian Carlo Menotti as the counterpart to his Festival of Two Worlds in Spoleto, Italy. Spoleto's little sister, **Piccolo Spoleto★** *(843-724-7305; www. piccolospoleto.com)* runs

©Spoleto Festival USA

Fireworks during Spoleto

85

Isle of Palms dock

©Wild Dunes Resort

Charleston holiday tradition. Held in early December, the parade features some 50 vessels, decked out with lights and holiday finery, which make their way from Mt. Pleasant down the Cooper River, and along the Battery to the Ashley River. A finale fireworks display lights up the sky above Castle Pinckney.

OUTDOOR ACTIVITIES

With all that water nearby and a climate that supports outdoor activity nearly year-round, the Charleston area can keep you busy golfing, swimming, fishing, paddling, playing tennis, or just lying on the beach. You decide how much or how little you want to do.

Beach It

The coastline north and south of Charleston is known for its wide sand beaches. Don't forget to bring sunscreen when you visit these beach parks *(see Beaches):*

- ♦ **Beachwalker County Park** –
  1 Beachwalker Dr., Kiawah Island.
- ♦ **Folly Beach County Park** –
  1010 West Ashley Ave.
- ♦ **Isle of Palms County Park** –
  1–14th Aves., Isle of Palms.

East Coast Canoe & Kayak Festival

Each April, James Island County Park is the site of a three-day-long weekend festival that includes on-water classes, demonstrations and lectures for novice and experienced paddlers. You can test out new kayaks and equipment on the water, courtesy of dozens of on-site vendors. There are cooking demonstrations and food galore.

A kids' cardboard canoe race in made-on-the-spot canoes is a highlight. *For details: 843-795-4386 or www. ccprc.com/ecckf.*

©Charleston County Park and Recreation Commission

86

The Charleston Angler

654 St. Andrews Blvd. (Hwy. 61). 843-571-3899. www.thecharlestonangler.com.
Area fly fishermen stop first at The Charleston Angler, which has everything from live bait to the best names in rods. The helpful staff, avid anglers themselves, will fill you in on recent fishing conditions and catches, and answer any questions you might have.

Go Fish

Water, water, everywhere—and that means lots of fish. Depending on the time of year, you can catch redfish, sea trout, tarpon, Spanish mackerel, jack crevalle, and more in Charleston area waters. For **offshore** and **inshore charters**, try the following operators:

◆ **Absolute Reel Screamer Charters** – *Depart from 2223 Folly Rd. 843-270-4464. www.follybeachcharters.com.*

◆ **Aqua Safaris, Inc.** – *Charleston Harbor Marina at Patriots Point. 843-886-8133. www.aqua-safaris.com.*

◆ **Fin Stalker Charters** – *Depart from various points. 843-509-9972. www.finstalker.net.*

◆ **The Reel Deal Charters, LLC** – *SC Aquarium Wharf or Remleys Point Marina. 843-388-5093. www.thereeldealcharters.com.*

◆ **Reel Fish Finder Charters** – *Moncks Corner. 843-697-2081. www.reelfishfinder.com*

If you want to go it alone, try one of the Charleston area's fishing piers:

◆ **Edwin S. Taylor Folly Beach Fishing Pier** –*101 E. Arctic Ave., Folly Beach. 843-588-3474. www.follyfishingpier.com. Hours vary; call or check online. $8 non-residents.*

◆ **Waterfront Park Pier** – *Cumberland St. to Tradd St. 843-724-7321. www.ci.charleston. sc.us. Open year-round daily 6am–midnight.*

◆ **James Island County Park Dock** – *871 Riverland Dr., on James Island. 843-795-7275. www.ccprc.com/jicp.htm. $1 park admission.*

©Charleston County Park and Recreation Commission

Young fisherman on the pier

FOR FUN

Greens Fees

Greens fees in the Charleston area can run as low as $35 for a city course to more than $200 for the resort courses, depending on the course, the season, the day of the week, and the time of day you play. Generally, greens fees are less expensive on weekdays and later in the afternoon. You'll often get the best deals in off-season, which in Charleston is from June to September and from December through January.

Hit the Links

Whether or not Charleston is, as it claims, the site of America's first golf course, is a matter of some debate. What's not debatable is that the area sports some great golf courses. Including the world-famous resort courses at Kiawah Island and Wild Dunes, the Charleston area counts two dozen courses open to the public. For a complete list of area links, check online at: www.charlestongolf guide.com.

Charleston Courses

Charleston National Country Club – 1360 National Dr., Mt. Pleasant. 843-884-4653. www.charlestonnationalgolf.com. Hailed for its beauty, this Rees Jones-designed course skirts marshland and natural lagoons.

City of Charleston Golf Course – 2110 Maybank Hwy. 843-795-6517. Opened in 1929, this well-maintained public course is just a five-minute drive from downtown.

Dunes West Golf Club – 3535 Wando Plantation Way, Mt. Pleasant. 843-856-9000. www.golf duneswestcom. Sister course to Wild Dunes, Dunes West is located on the site of historic Lexington Plantation.

The Links at Stono Ferry – 4812 Stono Links Dr., Hollywood. 843-763-1817. www.stonoferrygolf.com. The Battle of Stono Ferry was fought in 1779 on the grounds now occupied by this championship course.

Patriots Point Links – 1 Patriots Point Rd., Mt. Pleasant. 843-881-0042. www.patriotspointlinks.com. This is golf with a view of ocean-bound cargo ships, since Charleston Harbor's shipping lanes lie just offshore.

Resort Courses

You don't have to stay at Wild Dunes or Kiawah in order to play their top-notch greens, but if you're not staying at the resorts, you can't book tee times more than seven days in advance. (Off-season rates apply from December through February in the resort areas.)

Kiawah Island★★

21mi south of Charleston via Maybank Hwy. (Rte. 700) & Bohicket Rd. 800-576-1570. www.kiawahresort.com. See The Lowcountry Coast.

Kiawah claims no less than six golf courses (the River Course is reserved for property owners), including the world-renowned Ocean Course, which hosted the PGA Championships in 2012.

©LC Lambrecht/Kiawah Island Golf Resort

Ocean Course, Kiawah Island

Touring Tip

Kiawah and Wild Dunes resorts, as well as many Charleston hotels, offer golf packages that include lodging. Ask about package rates when you make your reservations.

Cougar Point Golf Course – *West Beach Village.* This course takes its name from the animals that used to roam wild over the island. Cougar Point was overhauled by Gary Player in 1996.

Oak Point Golf Course – *4255 Bohicket Rd., Johns Island.* Oak Point lies just outside Kiawah's gate on a former cotton plantation.

The Ocean Course – *1000 Ocean Course Dr., on Vanderhorst Plantation.* Golf Digest rated these Pete Dye-designed oceanfront links 25th on its list of 100 Greatest US Golf Courses.

Osprey Point Golf Course – *Vanderhorst Plantation.* Tom Fazio laid out the Osprey Point course around saltwater marshes and natural lakes.

Turtle Point Golf Course – *East Beach Village.* Rolling sand dunes edge part of Turtle Point's Jack Nicklaus design, with its strategically placed water hazards.

Wild Dunes★

Isle of Palms, 15mi north of Charleston via US-17 & Rte. 517. 888-778-1876. www.wilddunes.com.

The private resort offers 36 holes of championship golf *(see The Lowcountry Coast).* Both Wild Dunes courses were designed by Tom Fazio.

Harbor Course – *5881 Palmetto Dr.* This challenging par-70 course has four holes along the Intracoastal

Gator on the Green

Don't panic if you spot an alligator on the green; these critters are a common sight on many Lowcountry courses, especially those that border marshland (such as Kiawah and Wild Dunes). If you leave the alligators alone, they'll usually let you play through—just don't try wrestling a gator for your ball.

FOR FUN

Picnics To Go

Here are some places to stock up for a picnic:

Kennedy's Bakery and Market – *60 Calhoun St. 843-723-2026. www.kennedysmarket.net.* Everything in this neighborhood artisan bakery is made from scratch by hand, from crusty baguettes to gooey chocolate truffles. It's the perfect place to pick up picnic supplies.

©M. Linda Lee/Michelin

Bull Street Gourmet – *60 Bull St., at the corner of Smith St. 843-720-8992.* Bull Street's made-to-order sandwiches, soups and deli salads pair with craft beers and 400 labels of wine. All this plus imported cheeses are available to go.

Waterway, known to some duffers as the "world's longest water hazard."

Wild Dunes Links – *5757 Palm Blvd.* The top-rated Links course at Wild Dunes Resort on the Isle of Palms was designed by Tom Fazio in 1980.

Pack a Picnic

Charleston's peninsula has some primo places to picnic, complete with river/harbor views. For a break from sightseeing, try these:

Waterfront Park★ – *On the Cooper River at the end of Vendue Range. See Parks and Gardens.* Spread a blanket on the grass or settle into one of the wooden swings on the pier at this park.

White Point Gardens★ – *Along the Battery. See Parks and Gardens.* Set at the tip of the peninsula, White Point boasts water views.

James Island County Park – *871 Riverland Dr., on James Island. 843-795-7275. www.ccprc.com/jicp.htm. See Musts for Kids.* The park is equipped with covered picnic shelters.

Paddle a Kayak

Shem Creek Maritime Center, 514-B Mill St., Mt. Pleasant. 843-884-7684. www.coastal expeditions.com.

Paddling a sea kayak through the area's saltmarsh creeks, you can experience the Lowcountry in a way that few people do. Coastal Expeditions' 3-hour naturalist-led tours *($58/person)* include basic instruction and are suited to the novice. If you're proficient, you can rent kayaks and go off on your own *($38/half day, $48 full day)*. Either

Kayaking on saltmarsh creeks

©Charleston Area CVB

MUST DO

way, you're bound to see marsh birds and other denizens of the tidal creeks, as well as the shrimp boats that dock at Shem Creek.

Sail the Waters

To experience cool ocean breezes and a spray-in-your-face adventure, try one of these:

Schooner Pride – *Departs daily from Aquarium Wharf, at the north end of Calhoun St. Schedules vary; call or check online. 843-722-1112. www.schoonerpride.com. $34 adults, $26 children (ages 4-11).*
Hop aboard the 84-foot-long, 3-masted Class "C" tall ship, the *Schooner Pride*, for a look at Charleston the way the early settlers saw it—from the decks of their ships.
Resembling a 19C trading schooner, the 49-passenger vessel glides silently on its two-hour cruise. If you're feeling adventurous, the crew might just let you help trim the sails or even have a turn at the helm. *For more about harbor cruises, see p80.*

Cooper River Bridge Run

Registration required ($30; $40 after Mar 10). 843-856-1949. www.bridgerun.com. Charleston's ever-popular 10K race draws runners from around the US. Held each April, the run starts in Mt. Pleasant, crosses the Cooper River bridge—which is closed to vehicles for the race—and ends in downtown Charleston. A Kids Run is held the day prior *(see Parks and Gardens).*

Ocean Sailing Academy – *24 Patriots Point Rd., Mt. Pleasant. 843-971-0700. www.osasailing. com.* Why not learn to sail right now? You can join a small group of beginners and a certified instructor for a 3-hour lesson *($95 per person)* aboard an untippable 26-foot keelboat at this sailing academy. The hands-on experience is called "Be Part of the Crew," and is offered by the academy seven days a week *(times vary).* Call at least one day in advance to make a reservation *(Mon–Fri 9am–5pm).*

Schooner Pride

FOR FUN

FOR KIDS

From the aquarium to Patriots Point to a day at the beach, kids get a kick out of the Charleston area. Here are a few good ways to entertain the young and the restless while you're in town.

Middleton Place

©Middleton Place, Charleston, South Carolina

Family Fun at Middleton Place★★★

4300 Ashley River Rd. 843-556-6020. www.middletonplace.org. Open year-round daily 9am–5pm. Closed Dec 25. $25 adults (gardens & stableyards), $10 children (ages 6-13). Free for children age 5 and under.

Once a working plantation, Middleton Place *(see Plantations)* hosts a year-round schedule of events that capitalize on its past and will appeal to the whole family. Here are a couple of our favorites.

Plantation Days – *One weekend in Oct and one weekend in Nov (see website for dates).* It took a lot of work to prepare a 19C plantation for harvest time. Come see for yourself, when craftspeople demonstrate the different aspects of plantation life, including daily tasks, traditional African-American arts and Lowcountry foodways.

Plantation Christmas – *Mid-Dec 5:30pm–8pm; $15 adults, $5 children (ages 4-13); reservations required.* At Christmastime, come to Middleton Place for a special night of caroling, wreath-making, storytelling around a fire, and other holiday happenings at the Saturday **Family Yuletide at Middleton Place**. The live nativity scene stars animals from the plantation's stableyards, and artisans will be demonstrating their crafts.

Explore Middleton Place

4300 Ashley River Rd. 843-556-6020. www.middletonplace.org. Open year-round daily 9am–5pm. Closed Dec 25. General admission (gardens & grounds) $25 adults; $10 children (free for children under age 6).

Since Middleton plantation embraces a varied landscape of waterways and woodlands, it's only fitting that this natural wealth and beauty be shared with visitors. Through the Middleton Place Outdoor Program, you can explore the Lowcountry via bike, kayak, on foot along interpretive nature trails, and even on horseback. Go with a guide or take off on your own—the choice is yours.

MUST DO

Magnolia Plantation★★

3550 Ashley River Rd., west of Drayton Hall. 800-367-3517. www.magnoliaplantation.com. Open Mar–Oct daily 8am–5:30pm. Rest of the year daily 9am–4:30pm. $15 adults, $10 children (ages 6–12).

Children can enter the plantation's petting zoo *(open daily 10am–5pm)* with their parents to see pygmy goats and white-tailed deer on the grounds. There's a food dispenser at the entrance, so kids can feed the animals. On the **Nature Train** *(departs every half-hour; $8; children under age 6 free),* naturalists lead tours through the plantation's rich wetlands to spot animals like alligators; they also share the history and culture of the land.

South Carolina Aquarium★★

100 Aquarium Wharf, at the east end of Calhoun St. 843-720-1990. www.scaquarium.org. Open Mar–Aug daily 9am–6pm. Rest of the

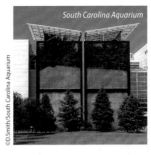

South Carolina Aquarium

©D.Smith/South Carolina Aquarium

year daily 9am–5pm. Closed Thanksgiving Day, half-day Dec 24 (open 9am–noon) & Dec 25. $19.95 adults; $12.95 children (ages 2–11). Free for children under 2.

If you've ever wondered what kinds of creatures inhabit the waters around Charleston, you'll learn the answer here. From seahorses to sharks, some 7,000 creatures and 12,000 plants fill the aquarium's 60-plus exhibits. Opened in 2000, the modern 2-floor facility overlooks Charleston Harbor and the Cooper River. Exhibits focus on seven watery environments found in South Carolina, from Blue Ridge mountain streams—a habitat for playful river otters—to Coastal Plains, where blackwater swamps harbor such denizens as alligators and diamondback rattlesnakes. Upon entering, check the day's

Henkel's gecko,
South Carolina Aquarium

©South Carolina Aquarium

Super Saturday

The third Saturday of the month, the aquarium hosts a special themed event *(11am–2pm)* packed with interactive fun for the whole family. Grab the kids and come on down—there'll be music, and activities such as kids' crafts, face painting, mask making, games and much more! It's free with general admission.

FOR KIDS

events for lively demonstrations, animal shows, and informative talks on topics of interest.

The Great Ocean

On the first floor, the aquarium's largest exhibit is two stories tall and contains more than 385,000 gallons of salt water—the water weighs as much as 457 adult African elephants! Watch 450 fish of 50 different species swim by, including a 220-pound loggerhead sea turtle, nurse sharks and porkfish, through a 28-foot-tall acrylic window. Stick around for the daily fish feedings *(Mon–Sat 11am & 3pm)* and educational dive shows *(Mon–Sat 11am)*. Don't miss watching the frisky otters get their breakfast in the Mountain Forest exhibit *(Mon–Sat at 10am)*.

Touch Tank

In the aquarium's Touch Tank *(on the first level)*, kids can have close encounters of the fishy kind with hermit crabs, sea urchins, horseshoe crabs, sea anemones, whelks, sea stars and other creatures called live invertebrates (animals without a backbone) that can be found on South Carolina's

Touch Tank, South Carolina Aquarium

©M. Linda Lee/Michelin

coast. Staff members are on hand to answer questions and tell curious youngsters about all these amazing critters.

Riverside Terrace

Just outside the aquarium, off the first floor, you'll have great views of the harbor and of the huge container ships that sail into the port of Charleston.
If you're lucky, you might even spot some of the harbor's resident dolphins. Kids can fuel up on

Lemurs

©South Carolina Aquarium

Madagascar Journey

The aquarium's newest exhibit showcases the African island that is home to 250,000 animal species, 70 percent of which live nowhere else on Earth.
Visitors can explore the plants and animals that inhabit the four varied landscapes of Madagascar, although the children's favorite focus will likely be the four playful ring-tailed lemurs.

MUST DO

Charles Towne Landing Founders Day activities

sandwiches or pizza in the Sea Turtle Cafe nearby.

More Fun on Aquarium Wharf

Fountain Walk – Located adjacent to the aquarium, the Fountain Walk encompasses a number of shops and eateries. Children (and adults, too) are sure to find something they would like to eat or buy.

Harbor Cruises – *See Musts for Fun.* The ticket office for SpiritLine Cruises is located on the lower level of Fountain Walk. Make the most of the Charleston area's varied waterways by taking time for a boat ride.

Fort Sumter Visitor Education Center – *On the south side of the aquarium. See Historic Sites.* Why did the North and the South pit brother against brother in our country in 1861? Find out the answer on a boat tour to Fort Sumter, one of America's most famous forts.

Charles Towne Landing State Historic Site

1500 Old Towne Rd. 3mi northwest of Charleston via US-17 to Rte. 171. 843-852-4200. www.southcarolina parks.com. Open year-round daily 9am–5pm. Closed Dec 24 & 25. $7.50, children $3.50 (ages 6-15).

The site where the first group of English colonists settled in 1670 *(see Historic Sites)* also has some cool things for kids to do.

Animal Forest – Bobcats and bison and wolves—oh my! Those are a few of the animals at this 22-acre zoo, in a natural forest setting. All animals you'll find in this forest are the same types of critters that would have inhabited the area when the first settlers landed here.

The Adventure – Docked on the Old Town Creek at Charles Towne Landing State Historic Site is the *Adventure*. This vessel is a full-size replica of a 17C trading ship. It is the type of ship that would have carried goods in and out of Charleston Harbor during colonial days.

FOR KIDS

95

Children's Museum of the Lowcountry

Courtesy of the Children's Museum of the Lowcountry

Children's Museum of the Lowcountry

25 Ann St., behind the Visitor Center on Meeting St. 843-853-8962. www.explorecml.org. Open year-round Tue–Sat 9am–5pm, Sun noon–5pm. Closed Mon & major holidays. $7/person (adults not admitted without children).

From toddler to age 12, kids will find a lot of activity in store at the Children's Museum. With a mission to spark a love of learning, the museum exposes youngsters to the arts, sciences and humanities through a series of exhibits/play

Paolo's Gelato Italiano

41 John St. 843-577-0099. www.paolosgelato.com.
What better way to end a visit to the Children's Museum than to go right across the street for a creamy gelato at Paolo's?
This Italian version of ice cream is made fresh daily and comes in a bunch of yummy flavors that both kids and adults will love—chocolate, caramel, strawberry, cappuccino, pina colada, Grand Marnier and more.

stations. They can dress up as a medieval monarch in Castle Stories, create their own rain storm in WaterWise! or dive into art projects. Don't worry, the kids won't realize it's educational—they'll just think it's fun!

Pirates! – Here children delight in donning pirate hats and brandishing mock swords aboard a pirate ship, while learning to tie knots like a sailor.

James Island County Park

871 Riverland Dr., on James Island. From downtown Charleston, take the James Island connector (Rte. 30) and turn right on Folly Rd. Take the next left on Central Park Rd., and left again at the stop sign onto Riverland Dr. 843-795-7275. www.ccprc.com/jicp. Open May–Aug daily 8am–8pm. Rest of the year, closing times vary. $1 (free for children under age 2).

Do the kids need some space to run? This 643-acre county park should do the trick. With picnic areas, ball fields, biking trails, and creeks for fishing, there's plenty of

Festival of Lights

If you're in Charleston around Christmastime *(mid-Nov–early Jan)*, take the family to the annual Holiday Festival of Lights, when James Island County Park creates a twinkling wonderland with more than 500,000 lights. Drive the 3-mile tour through the park *($12/car)*, but be sure to get out to visit Santa's Village, the Winter Wonderland and other interactive attractions of the park.

recreation here. Rent a pedal boat or a kayak, try scaling the 50-foot-high climbing wall, or go wild at Splash Zone *(see sidebar below)*.

Pitt Street Pharmacy

111 Pitt St., Mt. Pleasant (in the Old Village, off Rte. 703). 843-884-4051. www.pittstreet pharmacy.com. Open Mon–Sat 9am–6pm.

Enjoy a grilled cheese sandwich and a chocolate milkshake at the old-fashioned soda fountain in this unique pharmacy. It has been in business here since 1937, and still has a vintage look.

Climbing wall, James Island County Park

©Charleston County Park and Recreation Commission

Splash Zone

In James Island County Park. Open late May–mid-Aug daily 10am–6pm. Rest of May & late Aug–Labor Day weekends only 10am–6pm. $11.99 adults ($6.99 after 3pm Mon–Fri), $8.99 children under 42 inches tall (free for children under age 2). Splash Zone features a 200-foot tube slide, a 200-foot open slide, a 500-foot lazy river for tubing, and a Caribbean-themed water playground. Oh, and there's a regular pool, too (complete with lifeguards). Don't forget your swim suit.

©Charleston County Park and Recreation Commission

FOR KIDS

PERFORMING ARTS

Think Charleston is just a place for beach parties and shoreline strolls? Think again. This coastal beacon attracts an international crowd when it comes to performing arts. With such an impressive fleet of dance, theater, and music offerings, Charleston is worth its salt as a destination for must-see productions.

Spoleto USA Festival★★

Held in various venues in Charleston, late May–mid-June. Festival information: 843-722-2764. Tickets: 843-579-3100. www.spoletousa.org. Ticket prices vary depending on performance.

Every spring, Italian flair meets southern hospitality at this renowned festival.
Founded in 1977 by Pulitzer prize-winning composer Gian Carlo Menotti as the counterpart to his Festival of Two Worlds in Spoleto, Italy, the arts extravaganza showcases the best of Charleston—with its intimate size and grand spaces—as a setting for more than 120 performances. Yo-Yo Ma, Emanuel Ax, the Emerson String Quartet, and Philip Glass have all appeared in years past—and the list goes on and on.

A kaleidoscope of artistic genius, the Spoleto festival includes an entire spectrum of international talent spanning opera, jazz, visual arts and multimedia presentations, to name a few. From the downtown hustle and bustle, to City Hall and throughout historic theaters and churches, Charleston offers a diverse backdrop to the festival's delights. Additional venues include the early-19C campus of the College of Charleston and 18C **Middleton Place★★★** plantation and its gardens *(see Plantations)*.

Piccolo Spoleto★

Held in various venues in Charleston, late May–mid-June. Festival information: 843-724-7305. Tickets: 888-811-4111. www.piccolo

MUST DO

Opening Ceremony, Spoleto Festival USA

©Spoleto Festival USA

spoleto.com. Ticket prices vary depending on performance.

Not only does the city welcome top productions and performers—it also generates them. As the little sister of Spoleto (piccolo means "small" in Italian), the Piccolo Spoleto festival presents local and regional creativity through poetry readings, ethnic cultural presentations, children's activities, choral music, and more. Highlights from previous festivals include walking tours, outdoor juried art exhibitions, public art projects (such as *Larger Than Life* featuring 15 large-scale paintings displayed on prominent Charleston buildings), music block parties, improvisational comedy by Charleston's The Have Nots! *(see Nightlife)* and many more expressions of Southeastern culture. Venues range from the ridiculous (Starbucks) to the sublime (the French Huguenot Church), but the list is exhaustive and offers an excellent overview of Charleston's distinct traits.

Dock Street Theatre★

135 Church St. 843-577-5967. www.charelestonstage.com/ dock-streettheatre.html.

Concerts, operas, lectures and plays never ceased to entertain in this historic-district venue, built as a hotel in 1809 and reopened in March 2010 after undergoing a $19-million overhaul, including seismic reinforcement. Dock Street Theatre is home to **Charleston Stage Company** (CSC), South Carolina's largest stage troupe, which combines local talent with visiting actors from around the country to produce colorful shows like *Beneath the Sweetgrass Moon*, *Ain't Misbehavin'*, and *The Legend of Sleepy Hollow*. The 467-seat, 33,000 square feet theater boasts a lacy exterior New Orleans-style balcony and a rich interior, with black-cypress wall paneling, elegant arches and the carved wood bas-relief of the Royal Arms of England. It occupies the site where an earlier Georgian-style theater once stood.

PERFORMING ARTS

Courtesy of Charleston Stage

Dock Street Theatre

BOX OFFICE

Charleston Ballet Theatre

Performs in various venues.
www.charlestonballet.com.
843-723-7334.

Forget prissy tutus and prima donnas—this ballet company, founded in 1987 by artistic director Patricia Cantwell, prides itself on maintaining an energetic blend of modern and classical expression. Originally from Austria, Russia, the US, Canada, and beyond, the company's outstanding dancers form a vibrant team focused on refining and exhibiting their craft. Productions ranging from the delightful *Cinderella* to more explosive works such as *Firebird*, and *Mona Lisas and Mad Hatters* —arranged by Jill Eathorne-Bahr, the company's resident choreographer—dazzle audiences year after year.

Charleston Symphony Orchestra

843-723-7528.
Tickets: 800-982-2787.
www.charlestonsymphony.com.

Formed in 1918 as a loosely organized group that played mainly for friends, the Charleston Symphony Orchestra held its first formal concert in 1936 in Hibernian Hall. The professional symphony that now exists dates to 1970, when the group performed Charleston's first production of George Gershwin's folk opera *Porgy and Bess*, based on the novel by native son Dubose Heyward.

Today, a resplendent cast of musicians and guest artists (past performers have included Itzhak Perlman, Pinchas Zukerman, Marvin Hamlisch and Judy Collins, to name a few) fill every season *(Sept–Apr)* with sweeping sound and artistry. The CSO performs at a variety of venues, such as Gaillard Auditorium *(77 Calhoun St.)* and Memminger Auditorium *(see next page)*.

Charleston Symphony Orchestra

©John Zillioux 2012

MUST DO

The American Theater

456 King St. 843-853-0246
www.americantheater.com.
This World War II era movie house closed in 1977, but was renovated as an Art Deco-style dinner theater in the late 1990s. For a time, the venue welcomed movie goers with box-office films and even served food in the theater from the on-site concession. (Flip-up trays installed at each seat allowed for simultaneous viewing and munching.) No longer open to the general public, the American Theater

©Andrew Cebulka

now functions as a private-event venue, playing more to business people for meetings and conferences (though movies can still be screened here). A party atmosphere prevails in Stars Lounge, an upstairs hangout that can be rented for private parties.

The group, which includes 45 professional full-time musicians, brings the joy of music to the masses through a regular schedule of community concerts, school programs, and their major concert series: Masterworks, Backstage Pass Series, the Charleston Pops and the Chamber Orchestra. Do your best to try to catch one of their performances.

North Charleston Coliseum & Performing Arts Center

5001 Coliseum Dr. 843-529-5000.
Tickets: 800-745-3000 or www.
ticketmaster.com. www.north
charlestoncoliseumpac.com.

This oval arena takes on many shapes during the year: the 13,000-seat facility stages everything from sporting events—it's the home court of the South Carolina Sting-

rays East Coast Hockey League team—to energetic Broadway productions (*Les Miserables* and *West Side Story*), as well as performances by the Charleston Symphony Orchestra. James Taylor, Metallica, and the Ringling Brothers circus are among the acts who have appeared here. Check out the coliseum website or call for the schedule when you're in town.

Footlight Players

20 Queen St. 843-722-4487.
www.footlightplayers.net.

They aren't called "footlight" for nothing—this company has relocated more than three times since their inception in 1931, occupying the Navy Yard and Dock Street Theatre at different times over the years as temporary homes. Today the Players' performance venue resides in a large, renovated

PERFORMING ARTS

101

Theater, the Footlight Players

© The Footlight Players

cotton warehouse on Queen Street, making the most of the company's long-standing tradition to deliver top-notch performances— musicals, love stories, dramas—to enthusiastic audiences. Productions staged at this community theater star local actors in such shows as *The Elephant Man, Little Shop of Horrors,* and *West Side Story.*

Memminger Auditorium

56 Beaufain St.
www.spoletousa.org.

Officially reopened in May 2008 for the Spoleto USA Festival performance of the opera *Amistad*, the once run-down auditorium underwent a $6 million renovation overseen by local firm Huff + Gooden Architects. The "new" venue sports a sloping courtyard, scene storage, a garden—and air-conditioning, among other improvements.

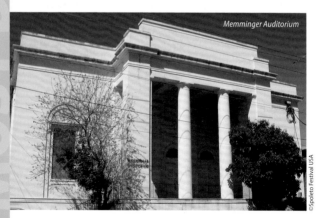

Memminger Auditorium

©Spoleto Festival USA

MUST DO

Sottile Theatre

©College of Charleston

Once part of an all-girls school, the building was designed as a WPA project in 1939 by Charleston architect Albert Simons. In the 1950s it was used for proms and other school activities. The auditorium was later renovated to host local events, but it was eclipsed as a performance venue by the Gaillard Auditorium, constructed in 1968. Memminger stood empty for years and in 1989 Hurricane Hugo blew its roof off. Yet its acoustics have remained excellent. It now hosts various performances and plans to publish a regular calendar of events in the near future.

🎭 Sottile Theatre

44 George St., on the College of Charleston campus. 843-953-5623. http://sottile.cofc.edu.

When you wish upon a star, you might end up in this twinkling theater at the College of Charleston, with its trademark saucer-shaped dome. Look up to marvel at the blue expanse of ceiling, accented with a sprinkling of tiny lights; then sit back and enjoy the brilliant performances of real stars on stage.

Built in 1922 by entertainment entrepreneur Albert Sottile, the theater served as a performance venue for films and vaudeville productions. With seating for 2,000 (the theater now has 785 seats), the Sottile [So-TIL-lee] was the largest theater in South Carolina when it was built.

A meticulous structural renovation in 1986 updated the theater's nuts and bolts, and added a spacious lobby area in front. The new look didn't end there; they spruced up the scene behind the curtain as well, with increased storage and dressing rooms. Further renovations in 2011 uncovered the remnants of original murals painted in the 1920s; the murals are awaiting refurbishing today.

With all the improvements, the Sottile continues to welcome an outstanding lineup of shows, including the Spoleto USA Festival and the Charleston Ballet Theatre. Past entertainment has included the Charleston International Film Festival, the College of Charleston Gospel Choir, ballet performances, an international piano series and magic shows.

SHOPPING

No wonder pirates loved this place! All the cultural delights and southern luxuries of Charleston are enough to make any treasure-seeking buccaneer weigh anchor. This seaport shopping phenomenon offers a wealth of loot, from antiques and modern art to designer labels and Lowcountry foodstuffs. What are you waiting for? Grab your gold doubloons (or greenbacks) and go shopping!

Old City Market

©Gwen Cannon/Michelin

MUST DO

Old City Market★★

On Market St. between Meeting & East Bay Sts. Open year-round daily 10am–6pm.

A three-block-long row of vendors' sheds, the historic market stretches from Meeting Street to the river along Market Street, with the new air-conditioned Great Hall in the middle. Every morning, stalls fill with vendors peddling an array of wares, including foodstuffs, sweetgrass baskets, jewelry, beach attire, handbags, crafts, and more.

Market Street

The blocks of Market Street adjacent to the Old City Market overflow with resort wear, fine art, souvenirs, shells and gifts.

A Shore Thing – *88 N. Market St. 843-853-4444.* From sundresses and T-shirts to sunglasses, hats and flip-flops, you'll find all things bright and beachy at this resort shop adjacent to the Old City Market. A couple of doors down *(#92)*, go nuts at **The Peanut Shop of Charleston**.

Fun Fact

The first market on this site (c.1840) was a meat market. Laws at the time required vendors to sell only fresh produce; at the end of the day, merchants threw any leftover meat into the streets, where it was devoured by vultures. Known as "Charleston eagles," vultures were so important for this purpose that they were protected by law.

Sweetgrass Baskets

As you stroll through the Old Market and along the streets in Charleston, or drive north on US-17 past Mt. Pleasant, you'll see black women making and selling a variety of coiled grass baskets. The coiled basketry craft came to South Carolina with slaves from West Africa 300 years ago. During the pre-Civil War plantation era, slaves winnowed rice and stored food in baskets made by coiling marsh grass with strips of palmetto leaves. In the early 20C, women began producing and selling "show baskets" made of sweetgrass,

©Doug Rogers/Michelin

a now-scarce dune grass found along the South Carolina coast. This art form, passed down from generation to generation, is now prized as a dying folk art. Labor-intensive sweetgrass baskets take anywhere from 12 hours to 3 months to make, a fact that adds to their value as well as to their price.

King Street★

Charleston's major commercial thoroughfare since colonial days, King Street still brims with shops, inns and restaurants *(between Calhoun & Broad Sts.)*. Chain stores like Talbots, Victoria's Secret, Gap, and Williams Sonoma put a modern face on shopping, while connoisseurs of all things old will delight in poking through the shops of antique dealers along King Street between Wentworth and Queen streets. Here's a sampling of some of King Street's interesting wares:

Shops at Charleston Place – *King St. at Market St., in Charleston Place Hotel. 888-635-2350. www.charlestonplaceshops.com.* From chain retailer to designer boutique, the mini mall in Charleston Place presents a litany of classy shops, including Chico's, Tommy Bahama, Godiva, Gucci, and Pandora. For the discriminating buyer, the Orient-Express Boutique in the hotel lobby proffers unusual—and pricey—gifts.

Croghan's Jewel Box– *308 King St. 843-723-3594. www.croghansjewel box.com.* Any Charlestonian worth his or her salt knows Croghan's. The revered family-run jeweler offers silver in all shapes and sizes in this tiny shop.

©Croghan's

Croghan's Jewel Box

Upper King Street

Once a run-down area with nary a place to eat or shop, upper King Street *(Calhoun St. to Mary St.)* is being revitalized with an array of trendy options catering to those with more disposable income. Browse through furniture, clothing and specialty stores here, along with chic art galleries and new restaurants featuring mouth-watering menus.

Christian Michi – *220 King St., at Market St. 843-723-0575. www.christianmichi.com.* Look in this tony Historic District shop for women's designer clothing, fine linens, and chic, colorful tableware, glassware and accessories for the home.

COS BAR– *201 King St. 843-793-1776. www.cosbar.com.* This new shop in the King Street antiques district is the place to go for the latest colors in make-up, high-end fragrances and rejuvenating skin-care products for both women and men.

Felice Designs – *424 King St. 843-853-3354. www.felicedesigns.com.* Designer Felice Killian makes jewelry magic with glass beads in every possible color and design combination. Her creative baubles include well-crafted necklaces and bracelets that are sure to bedazzle onlookers and wearers alike.

Le Creuset – *241 King St. 843-723-4191. www.lecreuset.com.* Many great cooks swear by Le Creuset's ceramic-coated cast-iron cookware. Here you can buy the entire line of these French pots and pans, which come in a rainbow of bright colors to match any kitchen.

Palm Avenue – *251 King St. 843-577-5219. www.shoppalmavenue.com.* Ladies, there's no need to be wallflowers when you can bloom in bright summer colors and flower prints at Palm Avenue. Here you'll find Lilly Pulitzers timeless designs. Looking for matching styles for mother and daughter? Palm Avenue can oblige in a range of vivid colors and designs.

Christian Michi shop

©M. Linda Lee

Yves Delorme – *246 King St. 843-853-4331. www.yvesdelorme.com.* Francophiles and lovers of fine linens will drool over the luxurious sheets and towels imported by Yves Delorme. Sure, a set of sheets here might set you back a pretty penny, but you're sure to sleep like a baby on this ultra-soft cotton bedding.

East Bay Street

Stroll along both sides of the street, from the Old City Market to Broad Street, for trinkets and treasures. Take a break from conspicuous consumerism at one of the many fine restaurants along this corridor *(see Must Eat).*

Fine art galleries are plentiful along East Bay Street in the Historic District. Here are some of our favorites:

Courtyard Art Gallery – *149 1/2 E. Bay St. 843-723-9172. www.court yardartgallery.com.* This co-op, one of the oldest in the city, features work by 14 local artists in a variety of media.

Gordon Wheeler Gallery – *180 E. Bay St. 843-722-2546. www.gordonwheeler.net.* Wheeler's shop showcases his limited-edition prints of golf, Lowcountry landscapes and Charleston scenes.

Lowcountry Artists, Ltd. – *148 E. Bay St. 843-577-9295. www.lowcountryartists.com.* This artists-owned and operated gallery features the works of 13 talented area painters, sculptors and photographers.

More Must-See Galleries

Numerous artists, including the nationally renowned Betty Anglin Smith, exhibit their creations in the city. For a lineup of galleries all in one place, check out **Gallery Row** *(Broad St., between E. Bay & Meeting Sts.; www.galleryrow.com).* Here are some other interesting galleries elsewhere in town:

- ◆ **Charleston Renaissance Gallery** – *103 Church St. at St. Michael's Alley. 843-723-0025. www.charlestonrenaissance gallery.com.*
- ◆ **Dog & Horse** – *102 Church St. 843-577-5500. www.dogart dealer.com.*
- ◆ **Pink House Gallery** – *17 Chalmers St. 843-723-3608. pinkhousegallery.tripod.com.*
  Smith Killian Fine Art – *9 Queen St. 843-853-0708. www.smithkillian.com.*

SHOPPING

Smith Killian Fine Art

©M.Linda Lee

If you have a craving for French truffles, chocolate bonbons and *pâtes de fruits*, make a beeline for this shop, set just off King Street and owned by third-generation French chocolatier Christophe Paume.

The Spice and Tea Exchange –
170-A Church St. 843-965-8300. www.spiceandtea.com. Whether you're a gourmand or just curious, you'll want to browse in this aromatic shop. The walls here are lined with jars of spices (feel free to open the jars and take a whiff) from allspice to zahtar. There are flavored salts, sugars and peppers too—not to mention myriad tempting tea blends, like the fruity Berry White.

More Must-See Shops
Charleston makes a career out of variety, and the area's assortment of boutiques is no exception.

Alpha Dog Omega Cat –
40 Archdale St. 843-723-1579. www.alphadogomegacat.com. A paradise for pampered pets— and their owners. Goodies include luxury collars and leads, and hand-painted pet dishes.

Christophe Artisan Chocolatier-Patissier –
90 Society St. 843-723-0575. www.christophechocolatier.com.

Charleston Cooks! – *194 E. Bay St. 843-722-1212. www.charleston cooks.com.* Need the latest in shrimp deveiners, cocktail muddlers or cookbooks by James Beard Award-winning Charleston chefs? Find all the high-performance kitchen gadgets here—as well as cooking classes in a state-of-the-art studio kitchen.

The Spice and Tea Exchange

SPICES – HERBS

©M. Linda Lee

Charleston Farmers' Market

On Marion Square, at King & Calhoun Sts. Open mid-Apr–late-Dec Sat 8am–2pm. Be sure to stop in at this fabulous gathering of local merchants. Tomatoes from Wadmalaw Island (considered the best around), local honey, okra, figs, butter beans, peaches, grits, even wine from Charleston's only winery *(see Musts for Fun)* make this a vibrant patchwork of flavors and aromas. Buy an armful of fresh flowers and take some local color with you!

©M.Linda Lee/Michelin

Charleston Crafts Gallery –

161 Church St. 843-723-2938. www.charlestoncrafts.org. Charleston's oldest craft co-op is a great place to buy sweetgrass baskets and creations ranging from art glass to hand-dyed fabrics.

Shops of Historic Charleston Foundation – *108 Meeting St. 843-724-8484. www.historic charles ton.org.* In this shop, you'll find a good selection of books about Charleston—pick up a copy of the historic district walking-tour booklet—along with classy gifts such as pewter julep cups, Charleston rice spoons, and pins, earrings and pendants fashioned in the design of Charleston gates. Look for the satellite shop in the Great Hall of the Old City Market. The Charleston Historic Foundation shop has now combined with the **The Shop of Historic Charleston Reproductions,** so you can also buy licensed replicas of mahogany period reproduction furniture here too.

Must-Have Souvenirs

No trip to Charleston is complete without a sampling of classic Lowcountry plunder, so put these on your list of souvenirs for the folks back home!

Sweetgrass baskets *(see p 105)* – A West African art form that's survived since the first slaves were brought to the Lowcountry, these woven wonders are handmade in traditional and modern forms.

Joggling boards *(see p 23)* – Since the early 1800s, these locally made benches have offered hours of bouncy fun.

Benne seed wafers – Munch on these legendary cookies, made from the "good luck" plant (benne is the African name for sesame seeds) brought from West Africa and made famous by slave descendants in the coastal region.

Charleston Rice Spoons – Even if you weren't born with a silver spoon in your mouth, you can fake it, thanks to Charleston's historic line of serving utensils. These long-handled silver spoons have been used to serve rice since the 18C on every "proper" Charleston table.

SHOPPING

NIGHTLIFE

The sun may slip beneath the waves on the horizon, but for those of you who shine after dark, never fear: this city isn't about to go to sleep. Whether you want to whoop it up or tone it down, Charleston's talent for combining local flavor with party flair means you'll have a good time at all hours. So put on your dancin' shoes or relax at a wine bar—whatever you do, don't miss the nightlife!

URBAN BARS

Bar at Husk

76 Queen St., Historic District.
843-577-2500.
www.huskrestaurant.com.

Clad in century-old exposed brick, this freestanding bar located next door to Husk restaurant is a destination in itself. Besides being a cool place to hang, the bar boasts a master mixologist who can whip up any libation you fancy, from historic to modern. Bourbon lovers will go gaga over the separate list of Kentucky bourbons, organized by town of origin and including the hard-to-find Pappy Van Winkle 23-year-old bourbon. A selection of Madeira speaks to the resurgence of this fortified Portuguese wine, which was all the rage in Charleston in the 18C and 19C.

Big John's Tavern

251 E. Bay St., Historic District.
843-723-3483.

If you're looking for a good time, you won't be disappointed by "Charleston's Best Dive Since 1955," as Big John's bills itself. Big John Canady—a former linebacker for the New York Giants—opened the tavern in 1954, never dreaming it would become a Charleston favorite. The convivial atmosphere means you're likely to make a new friend while you're here. If words fail you, no worries; nightly entertainment (including dance parties and karaoke) takes the heat off so you can let your hair down.

Blind Tiger Pub

36 Broad St., Historic District.
843-577-0088. www.blindtiger
charleston.com.

This landmark from 1803 takes its name from the illegal drinking parlors opened by boisterous locals in rebellion against the Dispensary Act of 1893. Called "Blind Tigers," the parlors operated on the premise of offering "free cocktails" to patrons who came to see the legendary (and imaginary) beast. The result? Happy drinkers and a frustrated government! Today the carousing carries on in honor of Charleston's colorful past.

Charleston Beer Works

468 King St., Historic District.
843-577-5885. www.charleston
beerworks.com.

Sometimes all you need is an old standby—and that's what you'll find at the Beer Works. This popular college hangout boasts pool tables, limitless beers on tap, and $2 pints from 5pm to 8pm. Check the online calendar for Monday's Trivia and Tuesday's crab legs. Buy-one-get-one-free appetizers and occasional live music mean Happy Hour lasts into the night here.

The Gin Joint

182 E. Bay St., Historic District. 843-577-6111. www.theginjoint.com.

Take a seat in this dark, cozy bar—or, if you prefer, grab a table on the brick courtyard out front—and swill an absinthe sour, a mint julep or a sloe gin fizz. The concept here seeks to bring back the heady cocktails of the pre-Prohibition era. Thus, you won't find any vodka drinks here, as that spirit hadn't appeared on the cocktail scene before Prohibition. In the late evening, you may run into some of the local glitterati, pairing their cocktails with items from the Gin Joint's selection of charcuterie and bar snacks.

🌿 High Cotton Maverick Bar & Grill

199 E. Bay St., Historic District. 843-724-3815. www.mavericksouth ernkitchens.com.

"High cotton" is synonymous with "livin' large," and this restaurant certainly goes the extra mile. Southern hospitality thrives in the sophisticated bar, while mahogany and brick create a warm, masculine setting, complemented by potted palms and heart-shaped straw ceiling fans in the restaurant. This is the place for decadent nights out, with a luscious menu

The Gin Joint

©M. Linda Lee

of Lowcountry fare and drinks crafted from the restaurant's own Maverick Private Label Liquors. Try a Charleston Cocktail: Maverick Vodka, Madeira, iced tea, lemonade and mint-infused syrup. Or sample your favorite varietal from the expansive wine list.

Go for live music nightly.

McCrady's Wine Bar

2 Unity Alley, Historic District. 843-577-0025. www.mccradys restaurant.com.

Part of the restaurant of the same name *(see Must Eat),* the wine bar at McCrady's makes an intimate spot to sample that "cab" or "zin" you've been wanting to taste. Tuck into a dark booth and whisper sweet nothings to your honey while you narrow down your choice of libations from among

NIGHTLIFE

The Have Nots!

Theatre 99 at 280 Meeting St. . Historic District.
843-853-6687. www.thehavenots.com.
Charleston may seem to be the epitome of
etiquette, but this multifaceted city holds its own
in uproarious antics, too. If you want to wear
yourself out with laughter, look no farther than
this hilarious improv troupe, along the lines of Chicago's famed Second City.
The infectious energy of these quick-witted actors keeps audiences howling
with interactive skits and ingenious spontaneity.

©Wes Fredsell

the 30 selections of wines by the glass, taken from the restaurant's award-winning wine list. If your love doesn't fill you up, pair your favorite wine with a selection from the daily changing menu of bar snacks. Ask about the schedule of wine tastings.

Music Farm

32 Ann St., Historic District. 843-577-6989. www.musicfarm.com.

This renovated storage depot is one of the hippest barns around, but the VIPs aren't your average livestock. Instead, the spacious, multilevel scene welcomes music lovers and musicians from near and far. Tones of simplicity, from original brickwork to exposed beams, keep the focus on the music—while the jazzy mezzanines and a giant mural keep it fresh. Previous performers include national acts Edwin McCain, They Might Be Giants, and Sheryl Crow, but The Farm is also known for staging the best local bands.

Social Restaurant + Wine Bar

188 E. Bay St., Historic District. 843-577-5665. www.socialwinebar.com.

Housed in an overhauled 19C warehouse, this place boasts a 4,000-bottle cellar and the city's largest selection of wines by the glass (a flight here is three 2.5-oz tastes). Complementing the wines are the likes of wood-fired pizza and ahi tuna crudo.
Libations and nibbles from the Happy Hour Menu, available weekdays from 4pm to 7pm, all go for just $4 each.

McCrady's Wine Bar

©McCrady's

MUST DO

The Last Resorts

Grand Pavilion Café & Bar – *At the Grand Pavilion, Wild Dunes. Open to hotel guests only.* Stroll toward the ocean behind the Boardwalk Inn and you'll find this cafe and bar. While you enjoy your drink, the little ones can have a cold one at the ice-cream shop.

Loggerhead Grill – *At The Sanctuary hotel, Kiawah Island.* Kiawah's luxury lodging offers several chi-chi places for a drink, but this is the only one right on the ocean that's open to the public *(grill open only to Sanctuary guests Memorial Day–Labor Day)*.

©Kiawah Island Golf Resort

Wet Willie's

209 E. Bay St., Historic District. 843-853-5650. www.wetwillies.com.

Young professionals frequent this dance club, where Thursday, Friday and Saturday nights, a DJ spins a mixed menu of dance music. If you'd rather sing yourself, go for karaoke on Sunday and Wednesday. Or just hang out, drink a beer and play pinball any night of the week. Wet Willie's frozen daiquiris are guaranteed to help you beat Charleston's steamy summer heat.

BEACH BARS

Check out these cool beach bars on sunny **Isle of Palms★**.

Banana Cabana

1130 Ocean Blvd., Isle of Palms. 843-886-4361. thebananacabana.com.

If Jimmy Buffet lived in Charleston, this would be his hangout. An outdoor deck with views of the ocean, a sand volleyball court, a putting green, and a band on weekends, make eating—and playing—here a blast.

Coconut Joe's Beach Grill and Bar

1120 Ocean Blvd., Isle of Palms. 843-886-0046. www.coconutjoes.biz.

Coconut Joe's beachfront upper deck is as close as you can get to the sand without being on it. There are drink specials every day, and live entertainment in season. Beat the heat with Joe's Dirty Rotten Banana, a concoction made by blending coffee liqueur, a fresh banana and vanilla ice cream. Or stop by Joe's for after-midnight piña colada pancakes.

The Windjammer

1008 Ocean Blvd., Isle of Palms. 843-886-8948. www.the-windjammer.com.

This is the place for bikini bashes, volleyball tournaments, bands and lots of beer. It's so popular that not even a hurricane can stop the crowds; after Hugo nearly demolished the original building in 1989, a new structure appeared in its place to the delight of beach babes and volleyball buffs. Live bands entertain here on weekends.

NIGHTLIFE

SPAS

Pounding the pavements in search of Charleston's fascinating history can be exhausting. Pamper those tired tootsies—and the rest of you—at some of the city's serene spas.

DAY SPAS

Earthling Day Spa

245 E. Bay St. 843-722-4737. www.earthlingdayspa.com.

The former Roxy Theater, a block from the Old City Market, now houses this progressive spa, whose staff blends the Indian healing techniques of Ayurveda with more traditional services. Float away into Nirvana with the package of the same name. It combines two Ayurvedic treatments: Shirodhara, where warm oils drip onto your forehead, and Bindi Herbal Bliss. In the latter, Indian herbs are used to exfoliate your skin, and warm oils are then applied to your body before sealing in the moisture under a steam canopy. Prior to your treatment, try one of the Pilates classes given at the studio here.

Stox & Co.

225 Willbrook Blvd., Litchfield Beach. 843-979-4233. www.stoxandco.com.

This spa has three locations in the area, and all three will make you feel pampered. Hair, nails, waxing and spray tanning are offered. The spa menu includes facials, body scrubs and massage. The Pure Bliss package is a 2.5hr facial and massage treatment for $283. While you're here, have a shampoo and style as well. Hatha Yoga and Pilates classes are available in private or group sessions.

Spa Adagio

387 King St., in the Westin Francis Marion Hotel. 843-577-2444. www.spaadagio.com.

"A Day at Spa Adagio" is the ultimate in pampering. Start with a sea-salt scrub, move on to a mud wrap, relax with a one-hour massage, then luxuriate with a facial, manicure and pedicure. There are also scalp, foot and even hand massage sessions available. And for men, the Gentlemen's Sport Facial is a 45-minute deep-cleansing treatment.
When, at last, you're ready to leave this historic-district spa, located in the lower level of the Francis Marion Hotel, you'll depart either with a spring in your step or slowly, in tempo adagio. Aaahh.

The Spa at Charleston Place

205 Meeting St., on the 4th floor of Charleston Place Hotel. 843-937-8522. www.charlestonplace.com.

You'd expect the spa at this Orient Express property *(see Must Stay)* to be something special—and it is. The Euro-style retreat, opened in 1999, offers a full range of massage, body wraps, facials, pedicures and manicures in an atmosphere graced by imported Mexican floor tile and blond wood tones. If you want to feel like a VIP, hop into the hotel limo that takes you to and from the hotel, and treat yourself to the day-long Champagne Dreams

The Spa at Charleston Place

©Charleston Place

and Caviar Wishes. You'll get a facial, French body polish, warm stone massage, lavender manicure and pedicure, and a two-course poolside lunch—complete with Dom Perignon and Ossetra caviar, of course. Men are welcomed here with such treatments as the Aqua Man and the Groom-To-Be. The adjacent health club offers a range of fitness classes as well as a heated swimming pool, sauna and Jacuzzi. Stay for lunch and sample the spa menu—it may be low on fat, but it's high on taste.

Stella Nova SpaSalon

78 Society St. 843-723-0909. www.stella-nova.com/.

Just the thing while you're in the historic district, Stella Nova sets

its upscale spa in a restored 19C house just off busy King Street. Stop by for an aromatherapy massage or a signature facial, or make a day of it and mix and match your choice of treatments. You might go for the 30-minute Stellar Salt Scrub, a body exfoliation using Dead Sea salts and pure plant oils; or Wrapped in Roses, a 90-minute treatment that rehydrates your skin with rose and chamomile oils. For skin that's been overdone by the sun, the Age-Defying Face zeroes in on wrinkles. Amino acids, vitamins and isoflavones work together to send you off looking and feeling younger. If you need sustenance, try the spa lunch, or the champagne and strawberries. Then before returning to reality, sip herbal tea and meditate in the spa's garden.

Urban Nirvana

8 Windermere Blvd. in the South Windermere shopping center, West Ashley; 843-720-8000. 636-D Long Point Rd., in the Belle Hall shopping center, Mt. Pleasant. 843-881-1160. www.urbannirvana.com.

The focus is on relaxation at this suburban day spa, which has locations both north and south of the peninsula. Massage

©Stella Nova SpaSalon

Stella Nova SpaSalon

Treatment room, The Sanctuary Spa at Kiawah Island

specialties here pamper everyone from couples to mothers-to-be and encompass styles that run the gamut from hot stone to wild lime blossom, a massage that employs an aromatic blend to relieve stress. Smooth and hydrate your face with a customized facial, designed specifically for your skin type; or indulge in one of the body wraps, which incorporate a range of ingredients from detoxifying seaweed to invigorating coffee.

DESTINATION SPAS

When you need more than just a day of pampering, head down the coast from Charleston to these spa getaways for a host of treatments.

The Sanctuary Spa at Kiawah Island Resort

In The Sanctuary Hotel, 1 Sanctuary Beach Dr., Kiawah Island, SC. 21mi south of Charleston via Maybank Hwy./Rte. 700 to Bohicket Rd. 843-768-6340. www.kiawahresort.com.

Opened in mid-2004 in Kiawah's new luxury resort hotel, The Sanctuary *(see Must Stay)*, this high-end spa takes on the ambience of a gracious Southern porch with its potted plants, trickling waterfalls, and chaise lounges for relaxing. Natural light floods each of the 12 shuttered rooms, where such treatments as the mint julep facial and the Lowcountry verbena body polish are inspired by the area's natural features: ocean, maritime forest and lush gardens. The spa's signature Body Wraptures will melt away your stress with a massage accompanied by warm grain- and herb-filled wraps. Golfers get their due with a Post-Round Massage, a full-hour treatment that soothes those club-swinging muscles and uses hot towels to enhance relief and relaxation .

The Cloister Spa at Sea Island Resorts

185mi south of Charleston at The Cloister, Sea Island, GA. 912-638-5148. www.seaisland.com.

This renowned spa takes it treatment cues from it its Sea Island location at the tony Cloister resort.

The Cloister Spa

©Karyn R. Miller/Sea Island

The Spa at Palmetto Bluff

93mi south of Charleston at the Inn at Palmetto Bluff in Bluffton, SC. 476 Mt. Pelia Rd., Bluffton, SC. 843 706 6615. www.palmettobluff.com.

Set amid bright gardens, live oaks and lazy rivers, Palmetto Bluff makes a perfect place to luxuriate. This top-drawer resort and spa is one of part of the line of upscale Auberge properties—as in Auberge du Soleil in Napa Valley, California. Sit back and enjoy a cocktail here—a bath cocktail, that is.

You're sure to find the formula that is just right for you among the infusions of aphrodisiac oils (for that bath *à deux*), detoxifying cypress and juniper, or stress-relieving lemon balm and jasmine. Of course, there's a full menu of massages, exfoliations, wraps and facials, as well as whirlpool tubs and steam rooms (bring your bathing suit for the latter two). Spa packages cater to everyone from Southern belles to avid golfers.

For deep relaxation, try a White Oak Soak followed by a full-body massage; or perhaps a Stone & Scent Concerto will restore your body's harmony. Gifts of the Sea uses seaweed masks, marine clays and an olive stone polish to restore your natural glow.

Energy work is available, too, in the form of myofascial release and Reflexology. Overdone by the sun? A Sea Island Essential Facial (60 or 90 minutes) is just what the doctor ordered!

©The Auberge Spa at Palmetto Bluff

The Spa at Palmetto Bluff

SPAS

MYRTLE BEACH AND THE GRAND STRAND ★★

Fun is the order of the day here. A 60-mile line of beachfront, the Grand Strand marches up the coast of South Carolina along US-17 from Georgetown *(60mi north of Charleston)* **to Little River. Sandwiched by the Intracoastal Waterway on the west and the Atlantic Ocean on the east, the Grand Strand's nerve center is Myrtle Beach. To the south lie the low-key coastal communities of Surfside Beach, Murrells Inlet (a great place for fresh seafood), Litchfield Beach and Pawleys Island. In addition to the lure of the sand and surf, the area draws duffers from all over the country to its 120 championship golf courses.**

The sights in this section are organized from north to south, beginning with Myrtle Beach.

Myrtle Beach ★

98mi north of Charleston on US-17. Visitor information: 843-626-7444 or 800-356-3016. www.visitmyrtle beach.com. Visitor centers at 1200 N. Oak St. and 3401 US 17 Business S. in Murrells Inlet (for visitor center hours and more practical information, see p 18).

The pulsing playground that is Myrtle Beach booms nearly year-round with people, traffic, and more entertainment options than you could possibly find time to do. But it wasn't always this way. Before 1900, this part of the coast was a quiet backwater. Enter the Burroughs & Collins Company, a turpentine manufacturer who built the first hotel on the beach in 1901. The wife of the company's founder named the area Myrtle Beach, for the abundance of wax myrtle trees

MUST SEE

Myrtle Beach

©Adele Lee Photography/Myrtle Beach Area CVB

MYRTLE BEACH

0 — 1 — 2mi
0 — — 3km

Alabama Theatre
Barefoot Landing
Alligator Adventure
Briarcliffe Acres
Barefoot Resort & Golf
Colonial Mall
Tanger Outlet Center
Arcadian Shores Golf Club
Lake Arrowhead
Waterway Hills Golf Club
The Dunes Golf & Beach Club
Pirates Voyage
Carolina Opry
Pine Lakes Intl Country Club
Myrtlewood Golf Club
International World Tour Golf Links
Ripley's Aquarium
Broadway at the Beach
NASCAR SpeedPark
Myrtle Waves Water Park
River Oaks Golf Plantation
Coastal Grand
Fantasy Harbour
Medieval Times
Arrowhead Country Club

Myrtle Square Mall
Myrtle Beach Convention Center
City Hall
Family Kingdom Amusement & Waterpark
Whispering Pines Golf Course
Springmaid Beach

ATLANTIC OCEAN

★★ THE GRAND STRAND

★ MYRTLE BEACH

MYRTLE BEACH INTERNATIONAL

Myrtle Beach State Park ★

Hotels
1 Anderson Ocean Club & Spa
2 Beach Colony Resort
3 The Breakers Resort
4 Hampton Inn, Broadway at the Beach
5 Island Vista
6 Ocean Creek Resort

Restaurants
1 Collector's Cafe
2 Croissants Bistro & Bakery
3 Hard Rock Cafe
4 House of Blues
5 The Library
6 Phillips Seafood
7 Sea Captain's House

that grew wild along the shore. After Hurricane Hazel razed the Grand Strand in 1954, the rebuilding boom included something new—golf courses. Throughout the 1970s and 80s, residential and commercial projects mushroomed, resulting in the megaresort you see here today—one of the fastest-growing areas in the country.

Myrtle Beach State Park

©Myrtle Beach Area Chamber of Commerce

Myrtle Beach State Park★

4mi south of Myrtle Beach on US Business 17. 843-238-5325. www.southcarolinaparks.com. Open Mar–Nov daily 6am–10pm. Rest of year daily 6am–8pm. $5.

Here's a beach at Myrtle without the backdrop of high-rise hotels and amusement parks. Developed by the Civilian Conservation Corps in the 1930s, the lovely 312-acre state park preserves a one-mile stretch of beachfront as well as one of the last stands of maritime forest on this part of the South Carolina coast.

Pawleys Island

Colonial rice planters had the right idea. They began coming to Pawleys Island in the 19C to escape their mosquito-infested plantations. Today shabby-chic Pawleys Island and its next-door neighbor, **Litchfield Beach**, cater to families who rent houses along this four-mile stretch of sand on the east side of the Waccamaw

Aerial view of Pawleys Island coast with vacation homes

©Ron Chapple Stock/Fotolia.com

MUST SEE

Touring Tip

Although Pawleys Island claims some of the prettiest beaches on the Grand Strand, it's difficult to access them if you're not staying on the island. Most of the land is private, and public beach-access points are rare.

River. With none of the high-rise hotels, amusement parks and other hoopla associated with nearby Myrtle Beach, quiet Pawleys enjoys a laid-back ambience.

There are no blaring radios, no beach volleyball, no noisy jet skis—just quiet sunning, swimming and strolling.

Huntington Beach State Park★

Across from Brookgreen Gardens on east side of US-17. 16148 Ocean Hwy., Murrells Inlet. 843-237-4440. www.southcarolinaparks.com. Open Apr–late Oct daily 6am–10pm. Rest of the year daily 6am–6pm, Fri 6am–8pm. $5.

Want an escape from the high-rise hotels and crowds at Myrtle Beach? Huntington Beach is the place. Huntington's three miles of beautiful unspoiled beach is a destination in itself, not to mention the acres of salt marshes, where more than 300 species of birds have been spotted.

Your first stop should be the **Education Center** *(open Tue–Sun 10am–5pm)*, where you'll find exhibits, park maps, a schedule of the day's events, and a boardwalk leading into the marshes.

The park is home to **Atalaya**, once the winter residence of Anna Hyatt and Archer Huntington, who founded nearby Brookgreen Gardens *(p 122)*. You can tour the Moorish-style castle *(open daily 9am–5pm; $1; floorplan with admission fee)*. There's camping here, and nature lovers can discover the diverse wildlife of the park's marshland ecosystem on their own along the site's trails, or via the various land and water tours offered through the 🚣 **Coastal Exploration Program** *(call or check online for schedule)*.

Atalaya, Huntington Beach State Park

Fighting Stallions by Anna Hyatt Huntington, Brookgreen Gardens

©Brookgreen Gardens

Brookgreen Gardens★★

3mi south of Pawleys Island off US-17. 1931 Brookgreen Dr., in Murrells Inlet. 843-235-6000. www.brookgreen.org. Open year-round daily 9:30am–5pm. Closed Dec 25. $14 adults; for children's prices see sidebar below.

Art and nature combine to form a stunning landscaped setting here. Opened in 1932 as America's first sculpture garden, Brookgreen is the love-child of artist **Anna Hyatt Huntington** and her husband, Archer, who created the gardens on the 900-acre grounds of an antebellum rice plantation. New attractions include The Oaks Plantation History and Nature Trail and the Offner Sculpture Learning and Research Center.

Huntington Sculpture Garden – This 30-acre display garden forms Brookgreen's centerpiece. Here, major sculptures anchor individual garden "rooms," serving as focal points at the end of long walkways. The noted sculpture collection, most of which is displayed outside in the gardens, contains more than 800 works of **American sculpture** (early 19C to present) by the likes of Daniel Chester French, Augustus St. Gaudens, Paul Manship, and Anna Hyatt Huntington herself.

Lowcountry Zoo – In a wooded expanse opposite the gardens, the zoo shelters bald eagles, great horned owls, foxes, white-tailed deer and other native critters. Many of these animals found a home at Brookgreen because they were injured and unable to live on their own in the wild. A cypress swamp is inhabited by alligators, and along the boardwalk in the

Touring Tip

Admission tickets to Brookgreen are good for 7 consecutive days. Daily garden walks, tours and special programs are included in the admission fee. Children ages 4-12 are $7; kids age 3 and under are admitted free when accompanied by an adult. Creek cruises *(see sidebar opposite)* are an additional $7 adults, $4 children. A tram runs regularly, transporting visitors from the gardens to the zoo and back. Otherwise, walking is the mode of transport (no vehicles allowed). You could easily spend a half-day here, so it's best to wear comfortable shoes.

Creek Cruises

One-hour cruises depart from the boat dock at the Lowcountry Center, Mar–Jun daily 11am, 1pm, 2pm & 3pm (no 3pm cruise Jun–Labor Day). $7 adults, $4 children (ages 12 & under). Evening cruises may be available in summer. Bring binoculars and mosquito repellant.

Kids and adults alike will enjoy a ride on Brookgreen's 48-passenger pontoon boat, which travels deep inside the preserve through blackwater creeks once used to irrigate rice fields. Now, instead of rice paddies, the wetlands are home to alligators, snakes, hawks, osprey, and a host of other creatures. Along the way, your guide will tell you about the labors involved in cultivating and harvesting the rice known as Carolina Gold *(see p 61)*.

©Brookgreen Gardens

Cypress Aviary, visitors might spot egrets, wooded mergansers and black-crowned night herons, among other species. At **River Basin Retreat**, an 8,000 gallon above-ground pool serves as a playground for the resident otters. Domestic plantation animals such as Red Devon cattle, Marsh Tacky horses and Tunis sheep are also on view; these heritage breeds are more characteristic of animals in the 1800s than of their hybrid counterparts of today. The zoo's newest permanent attraction is the **Butterfly House** *(open late Apr–Oct; $3 adults, $2 children)*. For a closer look at the zoo, catch one of the creek cruises *(see side-bar above)*.

Garden Eateries – Three on-site venues offer food service for lunch:
- The Pavilion Restaurant prepares soups, salads and sandwiches; and there's indoor dining as well as a shaded patio.
- The Courtyard Cafe serves up sandwiches, hot dogs, snacks and beverages, including beer and wine.
- The Old Kitchen has wraps, soups, desserts, beverages, and rocking chairs on the porch.

Diana of the Chase by Anna Hyatt Huntington, Brookgreen Gardens

©Brookgreen Gardens

Hopsewee Plantation

30mi south of Brookgreen Gardens off US-17. 494 Hopsewee Rd., Georgetown. 843-546-7891. www.hopsewee.com. Visit by 45-minute guided tour only, Feb–late Nov Tue–Fri 10am–4pm, Sat noon–4pm. Dec & Jan by appointment. Closed major holidays. $17.50. Grounds only, $7/vehicle.

Set on the Santee River, this Lowcountry indigo plantation is remarkable as the birthplace of Thomas Lynch Jr., who at age 26 was the youngest legislator to sign the Declaration of Independence. Lynch and his father, Thomas Sr., were the only father-and-son team to serve as members of the nation's Continental Congress.

Hopsewee Plantation

©Myrtle Beach Area Chamber of Commerce

South Carolina Treat: Boiled Peanuts

As you drive along US-17 through some of the little towns, you're likely to see signs advertising "boiled peanuts." Sold at off-road stands, this odd-sounding food is considered a treat by many South Carolinians. After being boiled in brine in their shells, the nuts are soft and salty. Many people think boiled peanuts are an acquired taste; decide for yourself, but first remove the shells!

Made of black cypress, the two-story Georgian home (1740), with its steep hipped roof and graceful double piazza (added in 1846), is now privately owned. Inside, you'll see fine examples of 18C and 19C American and European furnishings. The Tea Room serves lunch, hot tea and dessert *(10am–4pm)*.

Hampton Plantation State Historic Site

1950 Rutledge Rd., 16mi southwest of Georgetown off US-17 in McClellanville. 843-546-9361. www.southcarolinaparks.com. Grounds (free admission) open year-round daily 9am–5pm. House visit by 1-hour guided tour only, year-round Sat–Tue at 1pm, 2pm & 3pm. $7.50. Closed Thanksgiving Day & Dec 25.

Traveling for Health?

In 1776 the junior Thomas Lynch retired from political life due to health problems. After living at nearby Peachtree Plantation for three years, Lynch and his wife, Elizabeth, decided to take a trip to Europe, hoping that a change of climate would improve his failing health. In a cruel twist of fate, their ship was lost at sea on the outgoing voyage; none of the passengers survived.

MUST SEE

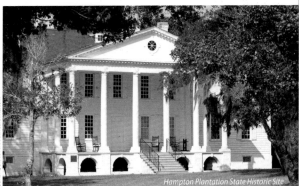

The Original Indigo Girl

Born to a British Army officer stationed in Antigua, Eliza Lucas (1722–1793) was 16 when her father, Lt. Col. George Lucas, moved the family to a plantation in South Carolina. The same year, Lucas was recalled to his post in Antigua, leaving his teenage daughter to run the plantation. And run it she did.

After her father sent her some indigo seeds from the West Indies, the young girl spent three years trying to cultivate the plant and learning how to extract the deep-blue dye—in great demand in England for military uniforms. Thanks to Eliza's successful experiments, Charleston's export of indigo mushroomed from 5,000 pounds in 1746 to 130,000 pounds two years later.

In 1744 Eliza married widower Charles Pinckney and assumed the management of several of her husband's estates. Their sons, Charles Cotesworth *(see Plantations, sidebar p58)* and Thomas, both distinguished themselves in early American politics. When she died in 1793, **Eliza Lucas Pinckney** was so revered that President George Washington, who had visited the plantation in 1791, insisted on being one of the pallbearers at her funeral.

A French Huguenot family by the name of Horry established this rice plantation in the mid-18C. Today the 274-acre Lowcountry estate showcases the elegant white Georgian-style mansion that began as a six-room farmhouse in 1750. You'll recognize the house by its columned two-story portico, added in 1791 by Daniel Huger Horry. Horry's mother-in-law, Eliza Lucas Pinckney *(see sidebar above)*, brought the design back from England. (Eliza made her final home at Hampton with her daughter, Harriott.) The last of the family line to occupy the residence was Archibald Rutledge, Poet Laureate of South Carolina, who died here in 1973.

The house remains unfurnished, and unrestored in places, in order to illustrate the original building techniques, such as the timber framing with its mortise-and-tenon joints, used to construct the house. The remnants of rice fields can be seen at Wambaw Creek.

Hampton Plantation State Historic Site

FOR KIDS

Think how disappointed the kids would be if you went to Myrtle Beach and didn't sample some of its many amusement parks. Here are a few of our favorites.

Alligator Adventure

©M. Linda Lee/Michelin

Alligator Adventure

4898 US-17, at Barefoot Landing, North Myrtle Beach. 843-361-0789. www.alligatoradventure.com. Open year-round daily. Hours vary seasonally; call for schedule. $16.99 adults, $10.99 children (ages 4–12).

If you haven't come across any alligators in your Lowcountry wanderings, you're sure to see some here—more than 800 of them, in fact. Along with garden variety and albino gators—some weighing as much as 1,000 pounds and measuring 15 feet in length—you'll see snakes, tortoises, otters and tropical birds as you explore the marshes and swamps. Watch alligator **feedings** *(mid-Apr–mid-Oct)*, and in the cooler months, when the alligators aren't eating, a trainer just might let you touch one in his or her presence.

Myrtle Waves Water Park

US-17 Bypass & 10th Ave. N. 843-913-9260. www.myrtlewaves.com. Open mid-May–mid-Sept. Hours vary seasonally; call or check online for schedule. $27.99 adults, $23.99 children (under 42 inches tall). Discount if purchased online.

Beat the summer heat at this 20-acre water park, where you can tube along a lazy river, play in the surf at the Ocean in Motion wave pool (that generates 8 different kinds of waves up to 4ft high), or rocket down the dark Turbo Twister tube slides at 50ft per second. The 32 water rides here include the tamer Bubble Bay for toddlers, and a 250ft-long river with a flow of only 10mph for little ones on skimmer boards *(children under 42 inches tall must have an adult with them)*.

MUST DO

126

Planet Hollywood

2915 Hollywood Dr., across from Broadway at the Beach (US-17 Bypass & 29th Ave. N.). 843-448-7827. www.planethollywood.com. If you're a film buff, you've got to visit this blue-green sphere, if only to see the décor. Every nook and cranny is crammed with movie memorabilia. The food centers on family-pleasing fare: salads, sandwiches, steaks, burgers and pasta. Kids will like the Chicken Crunch, strips of chicken with a sweet, crunchy coating; adults may appreciate the full bar. Be sure to take home a souvenir T-shirt.

NASCAR SpeedPark

US-17 Bypass & 21st Ave. N. Ext. 843-918-8725. www.nascarspeed park.com. Open Mar–Oct daily; rest of the year, call or check online for schedule. Online purchase $25.99 for unlimited track rides; $39.99 for full access. Per ride tickets range from $2-12.

South Carolinians love their NASCAR, as you'll see at this 26-acre amusement park—an official property of the National Association for Stock Car Auto Racing. The seven racetracks here range from the half-mile Thunder Road course *(drivers must be at least 58 inches tall)* to the 200ft Qualifier starter track for kids *(riders must be at least 40 inches tall)*. Mini-golf, rock climbing and an arcade are also on-site.

Pavilion Nostalgia Park & Carousel Park

Broadway at the Beach, US-17 Bypass & 29th Ave. N. 843-918-8725. www.pavilionnostalgiapark.com. Hours vary seasonally; call or check online for schedule. Rides $3.50–$4 each; unlimited rides pass $25. Discount if purchased online.

This family-friendly amusement park at Broadway at the Beach has several old-timey attractions like the pirate ship, tea-cup and kiddie motorcycle rides as well as a 1912 Herschell-Spillman carousel. The park harks back to the past with arcade games, old-fashioned funnel cakes and cotton candy as well. The giant wave swinger is a popular thrill ride. The midway has games to test your skills.

NASCAR SpeedPark

©Myrtle Beach Area Chamber of Commerce

Ripley's Aquarium

©Brian Gomsak/Myrtle Beach Area CVB

Ripley's Aquarium

1110 Celebrity Circle, at Broadway at the Beach. 843-916-0888 or 800-734-8888. www.ripleysaquarium.com. Open year-round Sun–Thu 9am–9pm, Fri–Sat 9am–10pm. $21.99 adults, $10.99 youth (ages 6–11), $3.99 children (ages 2–5). Discount if purchased online.

Toothy tiger sharks, Goliath groupers, and bright green moray eels are a few of the inhabitants here. Travel on the moving glidepath through the **Dangerous Reef**, where you'll be completely surrounded by 750,000 gallons of salt water and sea creatures from sharks to sea turtles. Meet critters up close at the Discovery Center touch pool. At Friendship Flats you can pet a stingray and see a bonnet shark. Stick around for a dive and feeding show *(ask at admission desk for schedule)*.

Friendship Flats, Ripley's Aquarium

©Myrtle Beach Area Chamber of Commerce

Carolina Safari Jeep Tours

Depart from Myrtle Beach area hotels year-round daily (reservations required). 843-497-5330. www.carolinasafari.com. $42 adults, $30 children (ages 6-12), $25 (under 6). Ready to see some species other than *homo sapiens*? Climb aboard these covered custom jeeps for a look at the wilder side of Myrtle Beach—the naturally wild side, that is. During the 3½-hour excursion, you'll drive to and walk around a Waccamaw Neck oyster bed, a barrier island, and several historic sites, including the churchyard where American poet James Dickey lies buried.

ENTERTAINMENT

From rootin', tootin' stampedes to jousting knights, family-friendly Myrtle Beach really knows how to put on a show.

Alabama Theatre

4750 US-17 S, at Barefoot Landing, North Myrtle Beach. 843-272-1111 or 800-342-2262. www.alabama-theatre.com. Shows at 7:30pm. Call or check online for concert schedule.

This theater presents a regular schedule of shows (Kenny Rogers, Bill Cosby, The Temptations, etc.) in addition to its signature musical and dance extravaganza, **One**.

Carolina Opry

©Myrtle Beach Area CVB

Doing the Shag

Born on Ocean Drive in Myrtle Beach in the mid-20C, the shag is South Carolina's signature dance. The four-count steps, which resemble the swing to the uninitiated, are performed to the tune of 120-beat-per-minute "beach music." South Carolina beach music (by such groups as The Drifters and The Coasters) embodies the rhythm-and-blues tunes of the 1950s that grew up along the coast here. Keep your feet moving and your upper body relatively still. Before you know it, you'll be shagging, too.

Carolina Opry

US-17 Bypass at N. Kings Hwy. 843-913-4000. www.carolinaopry. com. Call or check online for prices & schedule. No shows Sun.

The 2,200-seat Calvin Gilmore Theater presents music, dance and comedy in four live shows: the Carolina Opry, the Opry Christmas Special, Good Vibrations, and the LIGHT Laser Extravaganza.

Pirates Voyage

8901-B N. King's Hwy. at US-Bypass, North Myrtle Beach. 843 497-9700. www.piratesvoyage. com. Show times vary; call or check online for schedule. $28 adults, $24.30 children (ages 4-11).

Renovated in 2011, this new family-friendly dinner show promises swashbuckling adventure as two pirate crews battle for treasure, complete with acrobatics and animals. Dinner is four courses.

Medieval Times

2904 Fantasy Way, off Rte. 501 at Fantasy Harbour. 866-543-9637. www.medievaltimes.com. Hours & times vary seasonally; call or check online for schedule. $50.95 adults, $30.95 children (ages 3-12).

Here's another dinner show, only this one's a joust. Watch gallant knights on horseback battle for their honor—and the love of a beautiful princess. Kids will enjoy eating with their hands, just the way folks did in medieval times.

GOLF

Some 4 million rounds of golf are played in the Myrtle Beach area each year on 120 courses. While they're way too numerous to list them all here, the following picks will whet your golf appetite. For a complete menu of courses, check online at www.myrtlebeachgolf.com or www.mbn.com.

Barefoot Resort & Golf

©Myrtle Beach Area Chamber of Commerce

Arrowhead Country Club
1201 Burcale Rd., Myrtle Beach. 843-236-3243. www.arrowheadcc.com. Three separate 9-hole tracts here border the Intracoastal Waterway.

Barefoot Resort & Golf
4980 Barefoot Resort Bridge Rd., North Myrtle Beach. 866-638-4818. www.barefootgolf.com. Choose among the four courses here according to your favorite designer: Tom Fazio, Pete Dye, Davis Love III or Greg Norman.

Blackmoor
6100 Longwood Rd., Murrells Inlet. 866-952-5555. www.blackmoor.com. Lowcountry beauty abounds at Blackmoor, built on the grounds of an antebellum rice plantation along the Waccamaw River.

Caledonia Golf & Fish Club
369 Caledonia Dr., Pawleys Island. 843-237-3675. www.fishclub.com. Caledonia is consistently rated among the country's top public courses in the golf press.

Mini Golf
Sure, you'll get your time on the links, but what about the kids? With 50 mini-golf courses in the Myrtle Beach area, you'll be hard-pressed to avoid them, no matter where you go. Choose a theme, from prehistoric dinosaurs to pirate ships to erupting volcanoes. Just don't be surprised if the kids score lower than you do! *For a list of area courses, check online at www.golflink.com/miniature-golf.*

MUST DO

Greens Fees

Greens fees in Myrtle Beach can run as low as $30.50 to more than $200, depending on the course, the season, the day, and the time you play. Generally, greens fees are less expensive on weekdays and later in the afternoon. You'll often get the best deals in off-season, which in the resort area is from mid-November through February.

The Dunes Golf & Beach Club
9000 N. Ocean Blvd., Myrtle Beach. 843-449-5236. www.thedunes club.net.
This Robert Trent Jones course is private, but tee times are available for guests of partner hotels.

International World Tour Golf Links
2000 World Tour Blvd., Myrtle Beach. 843-236-2000. www.theworldtourgolf.com.
Playing World Tour's 27 holes is your passport to some of the world's best-known golf layouts.

Litchfield Country Club
619 Country Club Dr., Pawleys Island. 843-237-3411. www.litchcc.com.
Since 1966 live oaks and Southern pines have formed the backdrop for this Willard Byrd course.

Man O'War Golf Club
5601 Leeshire Blvd., Myrtle Beach. 843-236-8000. www.manowar golfcourse.com.
Golf architect Don Maples created the challenging par-72 layout around a 100-acre lake.

Possum Trot Club
1170 Possum Trot Rd., North Myrtle Beach. 888-999-9520. www.glensgolfgroup.com.
Reasonable rates and a helpful staff are benchmarks of this club.

Tidewater Golf Club & Plantation
1400 Tidewater Dr., North Myrtle Beach. 843-913-2424. www.tidewatergolf.com.
Often compared to the famed Pebble Beach Links, Tidewater sits high on a bluff overlooking the Intracoastal Waterway.

THE GRAND STRAND: GOLF

©Myrtle Beach Area Chamber of Commerce

Aerial view of the Man O'War Golf Club

SHOPPING

Don't wait for a rainy day to check out the numerous shopping malls and more than 300 outlet stores in Myrtle Beach. Go ahead, try these out for size!

Barefoot Landing

4898 US-17, North Myrtle Beach (adjacent to Barefoot Resort). 843-272-8349. www.bflanding. com. Open year-round daily; hours vary by season. Closed Dec 25.

Talk about all-inclusive entertainment—Barefoot Landing holds Alligator Adventure *(see p 126)*, the House of Blues *(opposite)*, and Alabama Theatre *(see p 129)*, not to mention 100 specialty shops, a handful of factory outlets, and more than a dozen restaurants. Set around a 27-acre lake, it's all made to look weathered, like an old-fashioned fishing village.

Broadway at the Beach

US-17 Bypass at 21st Ave. N. 843-444-3200. www.broadwayat thebeach.com. Open year-round daily; hours vary by season. Closed Dec 25.

You never have to leave this lakeside complex, unless you want beach time. Hotels, nightclubs, movie theaters, and attractions, including a carousel park are all here. The 11 nightclubs include Club Boca, for lovers of Latin dance, and Revolutions Dance Club for you disco hounds. Among the 20 restaurants are the Hard Rock Cafe and Jimmy Buffet's Margaritaville. Plus 100 shops and mini golf.

Coastal Grand Mall

US-17 Bypass at Hwy. 501. 843-839-9100. www.coastalgrand.com. Open year-round Mon–Sat 10am–9pm, Sun noon–6pm (holidays hours may vary).

The area's biggest enclosed mall features Southern department-store anchors Belk and Dillard's. Abercrombie & Fitch, Sunglass Hut, Victoria's Secret, and Foot Locker number among the 100 other stores at Coastal Grand.

Broadway at the Beach

©Myrtle Beach Area CVB

MUST DO

House of Blues

4640 US-17 at Barefoot Landing, North Myrtle Beach. 843-272-3000.
www.houseofblues.com. This shabby-chic music venue/restaurant may appear
to be a big weathered barn, but looks are deceiving. In a music hall lined with
tin from a Jackson, Mississippi tobacco barn, House of Blues hosts rock and
blues bands year round, such as Charlie Daniels, the Atlanta Rhythm Section,
and Catfish Lane. Oh, and don't forget the food. You'll see traditional Southern
accents in the generous portions of Creole seafood jambalaya, pulled-pork
sandwiches, buttermilk fried chicken, and cornbread served with maple
butter. Set your toes to tapping at the Sunday Gospel brunch *(9am–2pm)*—it's
fun for the whole family!

©Myrtle Beach Area CVB

The Market Common

4017 Deville St., Farrow Pkwy.
843-839-3500. www.marketcom
monmb.com. Open year-round
daily; hours vary by season. Closed
Thanksgiving Day and Dec. 25.

Sitting on 114 acres of a former
Air Force base, this upscale oasis
includes residential, recreational
and retail space. All the big-name
brands are here.

Hammock Shops Village

10880 Ocean Hwy. (US-17), Pawleys
Island. 843-237-8448. www.the
hammockshops.com. Shops open
year-round; hours vary by shop.

Fronting this collection of nearly
two dozen stores and eateries, all
connected by dirt paths beneath
tall pines, the **Original Hammock**
Shop *(843-237-9122; http://*
hammockshop.com; open Mon–Sat
9:30am-6pm, Sun noon–5pm)—a

Outlet Shopping

Looking for bargains? You'll find them in spades along the Grand Strand.
Tanger Outlet Centers – *US-17 at Hwy. 22; 843-449-0491. Second location (4635*
Factory Stores Blvd.) on Hwy. 501, 3mi west of the Intracoastal Waterway; 843-236-
5100; www.tangeroutlet.com. Open year-round daily; hours vary by season. Between
its two locations, Tanger offers some 175 outlet stores. From Adidas shoes to
Zales jewelry, you'll find a veritable ABCs of discounts here, encompassing
designer clothing, cookware, cosmetics, toys and much, much more.

The Beach House
©Gwen Cannon/Michelin

Pawleys Island staple since the 1930s—occupies a Lowcountry-style cottage.

Attached to it, the **Hammock Shop General Store** stocks beach clothes, books, birdhouses and countless other wares; don't leave without sampling a piece of the store's famous fudge, which comes in a variety of flavors.

In the adjacent shed, artisans craft the famous Pawleys Island's rope hammocks, handwoven since 1889 (see sidebar below). Popular stores **Affordables** and **Pawleys Island Wear** specialize in casual women's attire, and **The Beach House** features myriad gifts with a coastal theme. Long-time favorite **Island Shoes** carries must-have handbags and trendy women's footwear, and **Barefoot Elegance** stocks whimsies for home and garden. Also here are a Christmas shop, candy cottage, children's boutique, seashell shop, toy store, general mercantile, art galleries, candle shop and restaurants.

The Humble Hammock

What do you do when the grass-filled mattresses on your riverboat prove too hot and uncomfortable during the humid summers in the Lowcountry? You invent a rope bed. At least, that's what Captain Joshua John Ward did in the late 1800s. Ward, who transported supplies to the large rice plantations around Georgetown, South Carolina, came up with the idea of making a hanging bed of rope, to allow for greater air circulation. And it was portable, to boot.

©Myrtle Beach Area Chamber of Commerce

For more than one hundred years, his invention has remained unaltered; it still serves as the design for the Pawleys Island hammocks sold at the Original Hammock Shop today (see above). Take one home for those alfresco naps!

LOWCOUNTRY COAST ★

Named for the soggy coastal prairies that line the low-lying South Carolina coast north and south of Charleston, the Lowcountry incorporates quaint towns and a unique geography marked by acres and acres of water-laced marshes. Here you'll discover a host of wildlife along with a range of attractions from Gullah heritage sites to the upscale resort islands of Isle of Palms, Kiawah and Hilton Head. Whether it's peace and quiet or action you seek, you'll find it along the Lowcountry Coast.

©South Carolina Department of Parks, Recreation & Tourism, DiscoverSouthCarolina.com

Marsh in the Lowcountry

See maps pp 48–49 and on inside back cover. Sights in this section are arranged in geographical order, from north to south, beginning with Isle of Palms.

Wild Dunes ★

15mi north of Charleston on Isle of Palms. Take US-17 North to the Isle of Palms Connector (Rte. 517). When the connector ends at Palm Blvd., go left at the light and follow Palm Blvd. After Palm Blvd. jogs left at 41st Ave., take the first right (continuation of Palm Blvd.). Turn left across from 48th Ave. at the gate for Wild Dunes. 888-778-1876. www.wilddunes.com.

Bounded by the Intracoastal Waterway on one side and the Atlantic Ocean on the other, Wild Dunes sprawls out over acres of salt marsh, tidal creeks and two miles of white-sand beach at the northern tip of **Isle of Palms★**.

Long before a bridge connected this barrier island to the mainland, the Seewee Indians called the island home.

The first resort was built here in 1972 when the Sea Pines Company (which developed Hilton Head) built the Isle of Palms Beach and Racquet Club on 1,600 acres of land at the north end of the island. New owners added a Tom Fazio-designed golf course (Wild Dunes Links) in 1980, and four years later the resort's name was changed to Wild Dunes Beach and Racquet Club.

Accommodations here today range from the 93-room Boardwalk Inn *(see Must Stay)* to a wide variety of rental properties.

Wild Dunes tennis

©Wild Dunes Resort

Resort Activities

There's plenty to occupy your time at Wild Dunes. With golf, tennis, parasailing, kayaking, biking or just walking on the beach, there's no reason to be bored—unless you want to be.

Golf – Wild Dunes claims two championship golf courses *(see Musts for Fun)*, both open to the public.

Tennis – The tennis center here has a full-service pro shop plus 17 Har-Tru courts, 5 of which are lit for night play. Wild Dunes has been rated among the top 10 tennis resorts in the US by *Tennis Magazine* for nine years in a row.

Recreation – Adults can choose from working out at the fitness center, taking kayak tours, boating or parasailing. Day camps amuse the little ones with sandcastle building, scavenger hunts and field trips. For teens, the resort sponsors beach volleyball, pool parties and even a surfing clinic.

Kiawah Island★★

21mi south of Charleston. Take the James Island Expressway and turn right on Folly Rd. Go left on Maybank Hwy. (Rte. 700) to Bohicket Rd. Turn left on Bohicket Rd., following signs to Kiawah Island. Stay left in roundabout, then turn right on Kiawah Island Pkwy. and proceed to the entrance gate. 800-654-2924. www.kiawahresort.com.

Named for the Indians who hunted and fished here for hundreds of years before the first Europeans arrived, Kiawah Island embraces 10,000 breathtaking acres of maritime forest and pristine tidal marsh. In the 18C, the island was first owned by Revolutionary

Fun Fact

During the Revolutionary War, a cadre of 2,000 men under the command of Britain's Lord Cornwallis landed on Isle of Palms intending to cross Breach Inlet to Sullivans Island and launch a surprise attack on Fort Moultrie. The place where they made landfall is now the 18th hole at the Wild Dunes Links golf course. (Oh, and yes, the Patriot army was victorious in holding the British at bay on Isle of Palms).

Kamp Kiawah

Need some private time? Don't feel guilty about dropping the kids off at Kamp Kiawah. Youngsters ages 5 to 11 will stay entertained here with the likes of pirate adventures, crabbing, sand sculpting, crafts and contests. And it's all supervised fun. *Rates vary by season and program. Reservations required: 843-768-6001; www.kiawahresort.com.*

©Kiawah Island Golf Resort

War hero General Arnoldus Vanderhorst, who raised Sea Island cotton here. After the Civil War, the land knew a succession of different owners until 1974, when it was developed as a resort and residential community. Today Kiawah's 10 miles of uninterrupted white beach provide plenty of space for relaxation.

The Sanctuary *(see Must Stay and Spas)* is a luxurious oceanfront hotel and spa that opened in 2004 to round out the offerings of this world-class resort.

Resort Activities

If you're tired of sunbathing, try championship golf and tennis, bike the trails around the island or take the kids to the playground or the new kids' pool at 21-acre Night Heron Park. In case you consider eating to be a sport, there are 10 restaurants to choose from on the resort grounds.

Golf – Kiawah's five scenic golf courses, which include the world-renowned Ocean Course, were designed by some of the biggest names in golf *(see Musts for Fun)*.

Tennis – Two tennis centers on the property include 19 clay courts and 5 hard courts. There's even a practice court with a machine that will retrieve your balls for you. Tennis pro Roy Barth, a member of the Southern Tennis Hall of Fame, has been on staff here since 1976.

©Brigitta L.House/Michelin
Kiawah Beach at sunset

LOWCOUNTRY COAST

Wildlife, Wildlife, Everywhere

You'll share Kiawah's semi-tropical paradise with a host of winged critters: Flocks of egrets, great blue herons, osprey and myriad other waterbirds feed in the marshes in the early morning and at dusk. Plan a walk or a bike ride and don't forget your binoculars. You're likely to see deer on the island at any time of day—but especially after dusk—so be sure to heed posted speed limits. You'll also spy some good-size alligators sunning themselves on the banks of Kiawah's many ponds and waterways. They normally keep to themselves, as long as you don't bother them. Never, ever, feed an alligator! They become dangerous once they start associating humans with food; it seems that the reptiles' small brains don't distinguish between the food in your hand and your hand itself. And sluggish-looking gators can sprint at speeds nearing 15mph for distances of 50 yards—that's faster than you can run!

Catching fish with a seine, Kiawah Island Golf Resort

©Kiawah Island Golf Resort

Recreation – In addition to the island's 30 miles of bike paths (rent bikes at Night Heron Park), Kiawah's Nature Program hosts naturalist-led canoe trips, sea-kayaking excursions and bird walks. Two kids' pools, at Night Heron Park and West Beach Village, will keep little ones happy with slides and other watery fun.

Bohicket Marina Village

Just off Kiawah Island and right outside the gates to private Sea-brook Island, Bohicket Marina's location facing west on Haulover Creek makes it a great place to watch the sunset. While you're there, you can also browse the shops, have a bite in Rosebank Farms Café *(see Must Eat)*, take a cruise, go parasailing, or rent a boat.

Shops at Kiawah – Kids love to come to West Beach Village to get ice cream and browse in the gift shop; and the whole family can get breakfast all day at **Southern Kitchen**. Just outside the resort gate, **Fresh Fields Village** is filled with more shops, restaurants and a good grocery store.

Beaufort★

70mi south of Charleston via US-17 to US-21 South. Visitor information: 843-525-8500 or www.beaufortsc.org.

If Beaufort looks familiar to you, it's probably because the town has starred as the backdrop in so many movies—*The Big Chill, Forrest Gump, The Prince of Tides* and *The Legend of Bagger Vance*, to name a few. Its palmetto-lined streets, gracious architecture, moss-draped live oaks and flat tidal marshes make it the quintessential Southern setting. Make your first stop the **Visitor Center** *(see Touring Tip)* for a brief introduction to the town.

Bay Street, Beaufort's main street, is chockfull of interesting and colorful shops and eateries. At nearby **Blackstone's Cafe**

MUST SEE

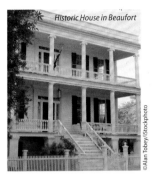

Historic House in Beaufort

©Alan Tobey/iStockphoto

Touring Tip

Leave your car at **Waterfront Park** *(Bay & Newcastle Sts.),* where a marina edges the Beaufort River. Bordering the park, Bay Street teems with shops, restaurants and lovely historic houses, most of which are privately owned. Walking-tour brochures are available at the **Beaufort Visitors Center** *(713 Craven St.; open year-round Mon–Sat 9am–5pm, Sun noon–5pm; closed major holidays).*

(205 Scott St., 843-524-4330; www.blackstonescafe.com), try a crab cake sandwich or a shrimp omelet *(see Must Eat).*

The walkable 304-acre historic district takes in the entire original town of Beaufort (pronounced BYEW-furt), chartered as part of Britain's Carolina colony in 1711. Spend a leisurely day here to get an intimate look at the wealth generated by South Carolina's 18C and 19C planter class.

The city's waterfront park spreads out along the **Beaufort River**. On Wednesdays *(May–Oct 3pm–7pm),* a farmers' market stretches from West Street to Craven Street.

John Verdier House Museum –

801 Bay St. 843-379-6335. www.historicbeaufort.org. Visit by 30-minute guided tour only, year-round Mon–Sat 10am–4pm on the hour. Closed Sun & major holidays. $10.

Washington may not have slept in this early 19C Federal-style house, but the Marquis de Lafayette did, in 1825. Merchant John Verdier's residence illustrates the "Beaufort style"—with its raised first floor, double piazza, T-shaped floor plan, and shallow, hipped roof—designed to take full advantage of prevailing river breezes.

Spanish Moss

You see it everywhere in the Lowcountry, hanging like fringe over the branches of live oak and cypress trees. A symbol of the South, Spanish moss is quite the misnomer: it's neither Spanish, nor moss. It is, in fact, an epiphyte, or air plant, which wraps its long silvery-green stems around a host tree and drapes from the tree's branches. The plant's narrow leaves are covered with scales that trap moisture and nutrients from the air. In the 18C, Spanish moss was used in many Southern households to stuff mattresses. The insects that were often trapped in this natural filler became known as bed bugs, as in "don't let the bed bugs bite."

©Brigitta L. House/Michelin

LOWCOUNTRY COAST

The Language That Time Forgot

Yuh duh talk en Gullah? (Do you speak Gullah?) On the sea islands of South Carolina and Georgia, they do. These islands are home to a small community of African Americans who speak **Gullah**, remnants of a language passed on from the early slaves who worked the plantations on the mainland. Kidnapped from their homelands and unable to communicate with whites or with each other, the slaves created a unique language based on their different West African tongues. Also referred to as Geechee, this Creole dialect incorporates the West African languages of Vai, Mende, Twi and Ewe with words from English, Spanish and Dutch, among others. Gullah strongholds remain on St. Helena, Daufuskie Island *(off the southern tip of Hilton Head)* and Sapelo Island *(Georgia State Parks offers tours of Sapelo Island; for information, call 912-485-2299 or check online at gastateparks.org/info/sapelo).*

©Red Piano Too Art Gallery

Penn Center National Historic Landmark District

6.3mi southeast of Beaufort on St. Helena Island. From Beaufort, take US-21 South and turn right at Martin Luther King Jr. Dr. 843-838-2432. www.penncenter.com.

Located a short distance from Beaufort, this historic complex makes an easy and worthwhile excursion. Now used as a conference center, the 17 buildings here recall the school established in 1862 by Philadelphia Quakers Laura Towne and Ellen Murray to educate Sea Island slaves freed

Touring Tip

Plan a visit on the second weekend in November to celebrate **Penn Center Heritage Days**, a three-day festival devoted to the unique cultural heritage of the Gullah people.

at the beginning of the Civil War, before emancipation.

York W. Bailey Museum – *110 Martin Luther King Jr. Dr., St. Helena Island. 843-838-2474. Open year-round Mon–Sat 11am–4pm. Closed Sun & major holidays. $5 adults, children $2 (ages 2-16).* Helping to

York W. Bailey Museum

©Wayne H. Heath/Michelin

MUST SEE

preserve Sea Island culture and history, this museum highlights photographs and African artifacts. It interprets Penn Center's impact on this coastal community.

Hunting Island State Park★

16mi east of Beaufort via US-21 South. 843-838-2011. www.southcarolinaparks.com. Open year-round daily 6am–6pm (9pm Daylight Saving Time). $5 adults, $3 children ages 6-15 (children ages 5 and under free).

True to its name, this beautiful barrier island was once used as a hunting ground. Now it's a 5,000-acre recreation spot that is South Carolina's most popular state park, attracting more than one million visitors each year. Palmetto trees and semi-tropical maritime forest edge the four miles of pristine beach. Anglers can cast their lines off the fishing pier (on the southern part of island), which extends 1,120 feet into Fripp Inlet. Nature lovers will want to walk the park's trails and look for sea horses in the man-made lagoon or try to catch a glimpse of pelicans, egrets, oystercatchers, wood storks and myriad other bird species that frequent this area. If you can't

Lighthouse, Hunting Island State Park

©South Carolina Department of Parks, Recreation & Tourism, DiscoverSouthCarolina.com

tear yourself away, reserve one of the park's 181 campground sites *(two-night minimum stay)* or its lone cabin.

Lighthouse – *Open year-round daily 10am–5pm (Nov–Feb 4pm). $2.* Confederate forces destroyed the 1859 lighthouse that once stood here so the Union army couldn't use it as a navigation aid. Rebuilt in 1875 (and renovated in 2003), the light towers 170 feet above the inlet. Climb the 175 steps to the top for a panoramic **view** of the heavily forested island and the expansive Atlantic Ocean stretching endlessly to the north and to the south.

The Red Piano Too Art Gallery

870 Sea Island Pkwy./US-21. 843-838-2241. www.redpianotoo.com. Mon–Sat 10am–5pm, Sun 1pm–4:30pm. A trip to St. Helena Island isn't complete without a visit to this gallery. A local enclave for Gullah art, it is packed with paintings, sculpture and folk art by 150 Southern self-taught artists. You'll get a good feel for Gullah culture here.

©Red Piano Too Art Gallery

LOWCOUNTRY COAST

Touring Tip

If you want to picnic at the beach, stop off along the way at one of the many produce stands, seafood shops or Gullah restaurants that line US-21, and get something to go.

Hilton Head Island★

30mi south of Beaufort via I-95 South to US-278 East. Visitor information: 843-785-3673 or 800-523-3373. www.hiltonheadisland.org.

With its resorts, golf courses and tennis courts hidden amid 42 square miles of natural marshland, beach and maritime forest, Hilton Head ranks as one of South Carolina's most popular vacation destinations. Two tennis academies and the Golf Academy at Sea Pines Resort help make it a year-round magnet for tennis players and golfers.

The island's namesake is English explorer William Hilton, who sailed into Calibogue Sound in 1863. Development began almost a century later, when the two bridges connecting the island to the mainland opened in the mid-1950s. Today Hilton Head's 11 planned residential communities, many named for the antebellum plantations that once occupied their sites, take up half the island.

Resorts

Here's a quick run-down of the resort communities that welcome vacationers:

Hilton Head Plantation – *7 Surrey Lane. 843-681-8800. www.hiltonheadplantation.com.* On the northern tip of the island, this 4,000-acre community has a beach on Calibogue Sound, four 18-hole golf courses, and a large marina.

Palmetto Dunes – *4 Queens Folly Rd. 886-380-1778. www.palmettodunes.com.* Here, you can choose your accommodations: rent a house or villa, or stay in one of two resorts—the Hilton Head Marriott Resort and Spa or the Omni Hilton Head Oceanfront Resort. Palmetto Dunes' three golf courses are all open to the public.

Port Royal Plantation – *10A Coggins Point Rd. 843-681-5114. www.portroyalplantation.net.* A mile-and-a-half beach borders Port Royal, which incorporates the site of the original Hilton Head bluff. While the houses are not available for rental, the Port Royal Golf Club and the Westin Hilton Head Island Resort and Spa are also located here.

Touring Tip

Most of the commercial amenities on Hilton Head Island are located along William Hilton Parkway (US-278). It runs 11 miles from the northern end of the island down to Sea Pines Circle. On your way in, stop and pick up a map and information at the **Hilton Head/Bluffton Chamber of Commerce Welcome Center** *(100 William Hilton Pkwy., just past mile marker 1)*. Note that addresses here can be difficult to find, given the island's strict ordinances that prohibit neon signs and limit the height of commercial buildings.

MUST SEE

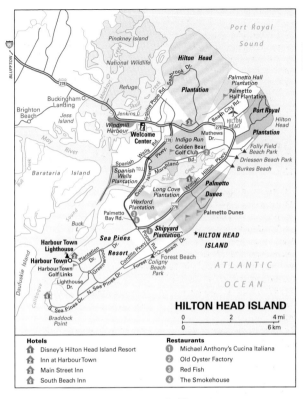

Hotels

🏠	Disney's Hilton Head Island Resort
🏠	Inn at Harbour Town
🏠	Main Street Inn
🏠	South Beach Inn

Restaurants

❶	Michael Anthony's Cucina Italiana
❷	Old Oyster Factory
❸	Red Fish
❹	The Smokehouse

Sea Pines Resort – *32 Greenwood Dr. 866-561-8802. www.seapines.com.* Located on the south end of the island, Sea Pines is the first (1957) and the largest (5,200 acres) of Hilton Head's residential communities. Amenities include Harbour Town village, 5 miles of beach and three public golf courses.

Shipyard Plantation – *Shipyard Dr. 843-785-3310. www.shipyardhi.com.* The 834-acre plantation embraces the Shipyard Golf Club, the Crowne Plaza Hilton Head Island Beach Resort , and the Van der Meer Shipyard Tennis Resort.

Golf

Hilton Head has more than 20 golf courses, 17 of which are open to the public. All of Hilton Head's courses are either located within, or associated with, one of the planned communities. Resort greens fees are on the expensive side, but vary depending on the course, the season, the day of the week, and the time of day you play. You'll often get the best deals in off-season, which in the resort area is from late-November through February. Here's a sampling of courses; for a complete list, go online: *www.golfisland.com.*

Sunrise, Harbour Town

©Leslee Alexander/Michelin

Golden Bear Golf Club –
100 Indigo Run Dr. 843-689-2200.
www.clubcorp.com. Walking is
allowed on this semi-private
course, named for its designer, the
Golden Bear, Jack Nicklaus.

Harbour Town Golf Links Course
– 32 Greenwood Dr., Sea Pines.
800-732-7463. www.seapines.com.
The renowned Pete Dye-designed
course hosts the PGA's Heritage
Tournament every April.

Palmetto Dunes – *4 Queens*
Folly Rd. 866-380-1778.
www.palmetto
dunes.com. Choose among the
wooded Arthur Hills course, the
lagoon-laden Robert Trent Jones
course, and the par-70 George
Fazio course.

Palmetto Hall Plantation –
108 Fort Howell Dr. 843-342-2582.
www.palmettohallgolfclub.com. The
Arthur Hills course here alternates
public/private every day with its
sister links, the Robert Cupp course.

Tennis

Tennis is quite a popular pastime
on Hilton Head; in fact, there
are more than 300 courts on the
island. Below are a few that can be
reserved by the public. Grab your
racquet and play a set or two.

Port Royal Golf Club – *15*
Wimbledon Ct., Port Royal Plantation.

©Leslee Alexander/Michelin

Harbour Town Lighthouse

149 Lighthouse Rd. 866-305-9814. www.harbour
townlighthouse.com. A Hilton Head landmark,
the hexagonal, red-and-white-striped lighthouse
marks the northern point of Harbour Town's yacht
basin. The working light is not operated by the
government; it was built in 1970 by the developers
of Sea Pines. Towering 93 feet above Calibogue
Sound, the light serves as a beacon for local sailors
and fishermen. Climb the 110 steps up to the
observation deck for a sweeping view of the island,
and while you're there, pop into the gift shop.

MUST SEE

Hilton Head Shopping

With some 200 shops on the island, you have no excuse not to pick up a few souvenirs for the folks back home. Sea Pines resort includes more than 20 gift and apparel shops at charming **Harbour Town**, on the north side of Harbour Town yacht basin *($5 entry fee if you're not staying at the resort; 866-561-8802; www.seapines.com)*. You'll find discounts on designer duds including Jones New York, Michael Kors, Polo Ralph Lauren and Kenneth Cole at **Tanger Outlets** on US-278, located at the gateway to the island *(the two centers are 1mi apart;1414 Fording Island Rd.; 843-837-5410; www.tangeroutlet.com/centers)*. If it's a mall you want, head for the enclosed **Mall at Shelter Cove** *(24 Shelter Cove Rd.; 843-686-3090; www.mallatsheltercove.com)*, where you'll find Belk, Jos. A Banks and Talbots.

843-686-8803. www.portroyalgolf club.com. The Racquet Club here features 10 clay courts and 4 hard-surface courts lit for night games.

Sea Pines Racquet Club –
5 Lighthouse Lane, Sea Pines. 843-363-4495. www.seapines.com. This highly rated tennis club offers 23 clay courts and is home to the renowned Smith Stearns Tennis Academy.

Van Der Meer Shipyard Tennis Resort – *116 Shipyard Dr., Shipyard Plantation. 843-686-8804. www.vandermeertennis.com.* Owned by tennis instructor Dennis Van Der Meer, this clinic-focused tennis resort boasts 20 championship courts, including the island's only covered and indoor courts.
The **Van Der Meer Tennis Center** is also located on Hilton Head Island *(19 Deallyon Ave.; 843-785-8388; www.vandermeertennis.com)*.

Daufuskie Island

From Hilton Head Island, follow US-278 over the Hilton Head Bridge. Take a left at the first traffic light onto Squire Pope Rd. Go about 2mi to the Daufuskie Island Embarkation Center, on the left. Ferry (www.daufuskiefreeport.com) departs twice daily for the island. No cars are permitted on Daufuskie island; only golf carts and bicycles are allowed (rentals of both available). www.hiltonheadisland.org/daufuskie-island.com.

Once known for its Sea Pines cotton and the oysters harvested from its waters, 8-square-mile Daufuskie Island provides a quiet respite from bustling Charleston and Hilton Head. Overnight rental accommodations are available. The island has a marina, local restaurants, a general store and a historic district. Two 18-hole golf courses offer views of the Atlantic: the Bloody Point links, named for a notorious 18C battle fought here between Native Americans and the British, will reopen in fall 2012 after renovation *(www.bloody-point.com)*. The Jack Nicklaus signature Melrose course is operating in a limited capacity until its resort *(see below)* reopens.

The commodious Daufuskie Island Resort was recently sold to a new owner, but an official reopening has not yet been announced. Its facilities include a 52-room waterfront hotel, a beach club with two swimming pools and a fitness center. Daufuskie's beach beckons visitors to its soft sands and gentle surf.

SAVANNAH AND THE GEORGIA COAST

It's only a couple of hours down the coast from Charleston to the romantic Southern city of Savannah, with its landscaped squares and eccentric ways. Another hour or so brings you to Georgia's fabled Golden Isles, a vacationer's paradise of golf courses, beaches and wildlife refuges.

SAVANNAH★★

Tourist information: 877-728-2662 or www.savannahvisit.com. For practical information, see p 17.

With its stately mansions, landscaped squares, Spanish-moss-draped live oaks and friendly residents, Savannah, Georgia, is a quintessentially Southern city. The city was born in 1733 when English army officer and philanthropist **James Oglethorpe** and a group of more than 100 settlers landed at Yamacraw Bluff above the Savannah River. One of 21 trustees to whom King

St. Patrick's Day in Savannah

You might think it's Mardi Gras when you see Savannah's St. Patrick's Day celebration. The squares aren't the only things that are green on March 17; the water in the fountains and the beer in the bars are dyed green, too. The celebration began in 1813 with the Irish Hibernian Society. Today the 2-hour-long parade and the River Street bacchanalia that follows attract hearty party-goers from around the country. *For details, call 912-944-6400 or go online to www.savannahvisit.com.*

Historic Houses in Savannah

MUST SEE

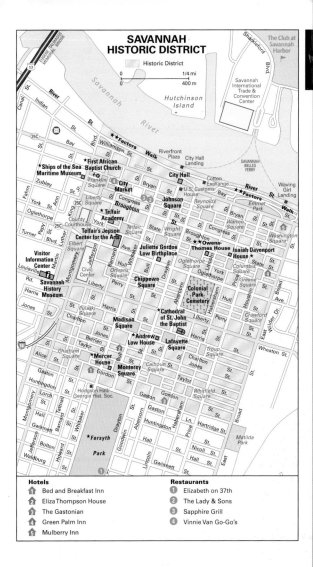

SAVANNAH HISTORIC DISTRICT

Historic District

0   1/4 mi
0   400 m

Hotels

1 Bed and Breakfast Inn
2 Eliza Thompson House
3 The Gastonian
4 Green Palm Inn
5 Mulberry Inn

Restaurants

1 Elizabeth on 37th
2 The Lady & Sons
3 Sapphire Grill
4 Vinnie Van Go-Go's

George II had granted the tract of land between the Savannah and Altamaha rivers, Oglethorpe envisioned the colony of Georgia as a place where the British working poor and "societal misfits" could carve out a living cultivating agricultural products desired by the Crown. In its early years, the region's economy, based on rice and tobacco, and later, cotton, fueled Savannah's growth as a port and a center for commodities trading. By 1817 Savannah's City Exchange was setting the market price for the world's cotton.

Of course, that all ended with the Civil War. When General Sherman finally reached Savannah in December 1864, city leaders surrendered without a fight. Sherman, acknowledging the city's beauty, presented Savannah to President Abraham Lincoln as a Christmas present.

Southern charm now pervades this historic city, which perches on a bluff above the river, as a testimony to visionary 18C city planning and modern historic preservation.

HISTORIC DISTRICT★★

James Oglethorpe's revered original city plan incorporated a perfect grid of broad thoroughfares punctuated by 24 grassy squares (three have been lost to urban sprawl). Bull Street cuts down the center of the grid, extending from 20-acre **Forsyth Park★**, with its graceful fountain, to the gold-domed City Hall.

Edged with handsome 19C examples of Greek Revival, Federal, Regency and Georgian architecture, Oglethorpe's streets

Touring Tip

Exploring the Historic District

Stop first at the **Savannah Visitor Center** *(301 Martin Luther King Jr. Blvd.; 912-944-0455; open year-round Mon–Fri 8:30am–5pm, weekends 9am–5pm; closed Jan 1, Thanksgiving Day, Dec 25)*, where you can catch one of the narrated **trolley tours** of the historic downtown. For a quick overview of the city's past, visit the adjoining **Savannah History Museum** *(912-651-6825; www.chsgeorgia.org; same hours as visitor center; $5).*

and squares are now preserved in the 2.5-mile downtown historic district *(bounded by Gaston St., E. Broad St., Martin Luther King Jr. Blvd. and the river).*

Factors Walk★★

West Factors Walk lines Bay St. between Whitaker & Montgomery Sts.; East Factors Walk is on Bay St. between Lincoln & Houston Sts.

Riverfront warehouses along Bay Street make up Factors Walk, hub of the cotton commerce in the 19C. Here cotton traders, called

City Hall

Separating East and West Factors Walk, 1905 City Hall *(1 Bay St. at Bull St.)* reigns as a vibrant local landmark with its 70-foot-high dome, covered in 23-karat gold leaf. City Hall stands on the site of the Old City Exchange, which set the market price for the world's cotton in the days before the Civil War. A **stone bench** in front of the building commemorates Oglethorpe's landing on this bluff in 1733.

Fountain in Forsyth Park

©Georgia Department of Economic Development

factors, would buy and sell from the bridgeways that connect the offices on the upper portion of the bluff—the two-story buildings that face Bay Street—with the warehouses on cobblestone **River Street** below. Walk down the steep steps to River Street, where restored 19C warehouses now contain a dizzying array of shops and restaurants. You'll find souvenir stores, candy shops, art galleries, a Christmas shop and an open-air market with 75 vendors.

Owens-Thomas House

The stately structure typifies the English Regency style; its tabby and coadestone exterior as well as the elegant interior—adorned with the likes of Duncan Phyfe furniture and a brass-inlaid staircase—have been carefully restored. Out back, the carriage house includes one of the earliest intact urban slave quarters in the South.

Factors Walk

Owens-Thomas House★★

124 Abercorn St. 912-790-8800. www.telfair.org. Visit by 45-minute guided tour only, year-round Mon noon–5pm, Tue–Sat 10am–5pm, Sun 1pm–5pm. Closed major holidays. $20 adults, $5 children (includes entry to Jepson Center).

The belle of Oglethorpe Square, the Owens-Thomas House is considered one of architect William Jay's finest works—and the only unaltered example of his surviving designs. Now administered by the **Telfair Academy★**, this house was completed in 1819 for cotton merchant Richard Richardson when the architect was only 25.

Andrew Low House★

329 Abercorn St. 912-233-6854. www.andrewlowhouse.com. Visit by 30-minute guided tour only, year-round Mon–Sat 10am–4pm; Sun noon–4pm. Closed major holidays & 1st 2 weeks Jan. $8.

In 1848 wealthy cotton merchant Andrew Low commissioned John Norris to create this Classical-style house with its elaborate cast-iron balconies. Low's son, William, married Savannah-born **Juliette Gordon Low** (1860–1927), who founded the Girl Scouts here on March 12, 1912. Located in back of the residence, the Lows' carriage house served as the first headquarters of the Girl Scouts USA—the world's largest voluntary organization for girls. Juliette Gordon Low died at Low House in 1927. Today Low family pieces and period antiques fill the rooms.

SAVANNAH AND THE GEORGIA COAST

It's Hip To Be A Square

Here are some highlights among the city's 21 existing landscaped plazas:

Chippewa Square – *Bull St. between Hull & Perry Sts.* Hollywood immortalized this square as the one where Forrest Gump sat waiting for the bus. A statue of Savannah founder James Oglethorpe by Daniel Chester French marks the center.

Johnson Square – *Bull St. between Bryan & Congress Sts.* Oldest of the city's squares, Johnson Square was laid out in 1733.

Lafayette Square – *Abercorn St. between E. Harris & E. Charleton Sts.* A three-tiered fountain centers this square, named for the Marquis de Lafayette.

Madison Square – *Bull St. between W. Harris & W. Charleton Sts.* Named for President James Madison, this plaza holds a statue of a Revolutionary War hero.

Monterey Square – *Bull St. between Taylor & Gordon Sts.* Monterey Square boasts a monument (1854) honoring General Casimir Pulaski, who was mortally wounded near this spot during the 1779 Siege of Savannah.

Cathedral of St. John the Baptist

©Georgia Department of Economic Development

Cathedral of St. John the Baptist★

222 E. Harris St. 912-233-4709. www.savannahcathedral.org. Open year-round Mon–Fri 9am–5pm.

You'll recognize the seat of Savannah's Catholic diocese by the twin spires that tower over the historic district. Dedicated in 1876, this French Gothic cathedral dates back to a parish established in Savannah in the late 1700s. Step inside to see the results of the

four-year restoration (completed in 2000) that returned the cathedral's Austrian stained-glass windows and Italian marble altar to their former glory.

Isaiah Davenport House★

324 E. State St. 912-236-8097. www.davenporthousemuseum.org. Visit by 30-minute guided tour only, year-round Mon–Sat 10am–4pm, Sun 1pm–4pm (last tour starts at 4pm). $8.

Designed by Rhode Island master builder Isaiah Davenport, this two-story brick Federal structure was completed in 1820. When threatened by demolition in the

Isaiah Davenport House

©M. Linda Lee/Michelin

1950s, community efforts saved it and established the Historic Savannah Foundation, a grassroots organization that has been key in rejuvenating the historic district.

Ships of the Sea Maritime Museum★

41 Martin Luther King Jr. Blvd. 912-232-1511. www.shipsofthe sea.org. Open year-round Tue–Sun 10am–5pm. Closed Mon & major holidays. $8.

A block west of City Market, a charming garden invites visitors into Scarbrough House, an 1819 Regency villa designed by famed English architect William Jay. Today the villa houses a maritime museum, which presents nautical history and seafaring culture through artifacts, paintings and model ships from the earliest days of sail to World War II.

Telfair Academy★

121 Barnard St. 912-232-1177. www.telfair.org. Open year-round Mon noon–5pm, Tue–Sat 10am– 5pm, Sun 1pm–5pm. Closed major holidays. $20 adults, $5 children (includes entry to Owens-Thomas House and Jepson Center).

Another creation of William Jay, the Regency-style mansion was built in 1818 as the home of Alexander Telfair. The expanded structure now houses 19C and 20C American and European paintings and portraiture, including works by members of the Ash Can school— Robert Henri, George Luks and George Bellows.

Located on the entrance level was Telfair's reception room, the Octagon Room, with its 19C Grecian couches and faux oak paneling; and the Dining Room, showcasing a Duncan Phyfe

Telfair Academy

©Georgia Department of Economic Development

Broughton Street Shopping

Let's face it, shopping along the riverfront is fine if you want T-shirts and Savannah-emblazoned souvenirs, but you'll find more interesting shops along Broughton Street, from Bull Street to Martin Luther King Jr. Boulevard. Here are a few examples:

Go Fish – *106 W. Broughton St. 912-554-3836. www.shopgofish.com.* The casual women's clothing here is made by indigenous people of developing nations.

Clipper Trading Company – *201 W. Broughton St. 912-238-3660. www.clipper trading.com.* Antiques and Asian imports fill this former five-and-dime store.

Zia Boutique – *325 W. Broughton St. 912-233-3237. www.ziaboutique.com.* Find exotic, colorful jewelry and gifts inspired by the Kenyan owner's world travels.

Midnight in the Garden of Good and Evil

429 Bull St. 912-236-6352. www.mercerhouse.com. Visit by 30-min guided tour only, year-round Mon–Sat 10:30am–4pm, Sun noon–4pm. $12.50. Tickets at Mercer House Carriage Shop, 430 Whitaker St. (Mon–Sat 10am–5pm, Sun 10:30am–4:30pm). A stately Italianate mansion overlooking Monterey Square, the c.1868 **Mercer Williams House★**—designed by New York architect John Norris—became famous as a crime scene.

It was in this house in 1981 that resident antiques dealer Jim Williams was accused of fatally shooting 21-year-old Danny Hansford. Williams' murder trial set staid Savannah on its ear, and was later immortalized in John Berendt's best-selling 1994 book *Midnight in the Garden of Good and Evil*. Both the book and the movie that followed in 1997 painted a vivid picture of Savannah's eccentric populace. The most recognized icon from the book is, perhaps, the sculpture *Bird Girl* (1938), which appears on the book's cover. The work of Sylvia Shaw Judson, the statue stands in the Telfair Academy.

mahogany sideboard and early 19C English silver.

Next door, the modern 64,000-square-foot **Jepson Center** *(Sun–Mon noon–5pm, Tue–Sat 10am–5pm, Thu til 8pm)* was designed for Telfair by renowned architect Moshe Safdie. It houses the academy's collection of 20C and 21C art, including a prestigious array of works on paper by major artists of the past 50 years.

Fort Pulaski National Monument★

14mi east of downtown Savannah via US-80, on Tybee Island. 912-786-5787. www.nps.gov/fopu. Open year-round daily 9am–5:30pm (later summer). Closed Jan 1, Thanksgiving Day, Dec 25. $5.

Named for Revolutionary War hero **Casimir Pulaski**, who lost his life defending the city of Savannah against the British, Fort Pulaski

Fort Pulaski Natonal Monument

was built between 1833 and 1847. The battery saw most of its action during the Civil War, when Confederate troops sieged the fort even before Georgia seceded from the Union. In April 1862, Union forces recaptured the fort, using their experimental rifled cannon. They quickly sealed off the port of Savannah and held the fort for the rest of the war.

Fort Pulaski was declared a national monument in 1924. Today you can tour its restored ramparts, complete with cannon, moat and drawbridge. The 5,600-acre site includes picnic grounds and nature trails, with views of the Atlantic Ocean in the distance.

City Market

Bounded by Montgomery, Bryan, Congress and Barnard Sts. 912-232-4903. www.savannahcitymarket.com.

City Market

©M. Linda Lee/Michelin

At City Market, listen to live music, catch a carriage tour, sample the shops or relax at the outdoor cafes at this lively marketplace. Across from the market, **First African Baptist Church★** *(23 Montgomery St.; 912-233-6597; www.firstafricanbc.com)* is considered the oldest black church (1773) in North America; it was founded by freed slave George Leile. The current structure was built in 1859 by members of the congregation.

Colonial Park Cemetery

Entrance at Abercorn & E. Oglethorpe Sts. 912-944-0455. Open year-round daily 8am–5pm.

Inside the gates of Colonial Park you'll find some of Savannah's most distinguished citizens— deceased, of course. Savannah's second cemetery opened in 1750; the last body was buried here in 1853. Tucked amid the live oaks you'll find the graves of James Habersham, acting Royal Governor of the Province of Georgia from 1771–73; naval hero Capt. Denis Cottineau, who fought with John Paul Jones in 1779; and renowned 18C miniaturist Edward Greene Malbone. The cemetery has been a park since 1896.

Juliette Gordon Low Birthplace

10 E. Oglethorpe Ave. 912-233-4501. www.juliettegordonlow birthplace.org. Vist by 30-minute guided tour only, Mar–Oct Mon–Sat 10am–4pm, Sun 11am–4pm. Rest of the year, no tours Wed. Closed major holidays and 1st 2 weeks in Jan. $8.

The founder of the Girl Scouts was born in this house in 1860. Known as Daisy, Low was the second of six children of cotton factor William Gordon II and his wife, Eleanor. The 1821 English Regency-style house has been painstakingly restored to reflect the year 1886, when Juliette Gordon married William Mackay Low.

GEORGIA'S GOLDEN ISLES ★

Tourist information: 912-265-0620 or 800-933-2627; www.goldenisles.com.
To reach the Golden Isles from Savannah, travel south on I-95 from Savannah
to US-17 South. For practical information, see p 17.

**Strung like shining beads along Georgia's Atlantic Coast, the Golden
Isles—Sea Island, St. Simons Island, private Little St. Simons Island**
(see p 157), **and Jekyll Island—lie amid a setting of gold-green marshes,
diamond-white sands and lapis-blue waters. These popular destinations, located 70 miles south of Savannah and boasting an average
annual temperature of 68°F, attract thousands of visitors each year
to play on the area's golf courses and tennis courts, visit its historic
resorts, and relax on its wide sandy beaches.**

Jekyll Island ★★

*From I-95, take Exit 29 and follow
US-17 to the Jekyll Causeway. Jekyll
Island Welcome Center is located
on the causeway (901 Downing
Musgrove Causeway). 912-635-
3636. www.jekyllisland.com.
Open year-round daily 9am–5pm.
There's a $3/vehicle fee to drive
onto the island.*

Dubbed "Georgia's Jewel," Jekyll
Island grew up as a playground
for America's millionaires—do the
names Gould, Goodyear, Pulitzer
and Rockefeller ring a bell? These
men, and other East Coast captains

of industry, formed a consortium in
1886 and purchased the island for
$125,000. Here in 1887, consortium
members—who called themselves
the Jekyll Island Club—hired
architect Charles Alexander to
build a 60-room clubhouse (now
the Jekyll Island Club Hotel).
The wealthy financiers soon
supplemented their clubhouse
with "cottages," as they called
their anything-but-modest winter
retreats, which ranged up to 8,000
square feet in size.
In 1942, World War II put an end
to the playtime, when the club
closed. In 1947 the State of Georgia

Jekyll Island beach

©Georgia Department of Economic Development

MUST SEE

Brunswick Stew

First created in Brunswick, Georgia—the commercial hub of the Golden Isles and an important port in its own right—delectable Brunswick stew combines chicken, beef and pork, slow-simmered with local vegetables (tomatoes, butter beans, corn, potatoes and okra), herbs and spices. It's often served with fresh local shrimp, crab and oysters, and appears on many menus throughout the area. Be sure to sample some while you're in the area.

Jekyll Island Club
©M.Linda Lee/Michelin

facility that is open to the public. Wander around at your leisure, or take a guided tram tour.

purchased the island, which today preserves Jekyll's historic structures within the 240-acre Jekyll Island Historic District, now a National Historic Landmark. The ocean side of the island is lined with hotels and 🏖 **beautiful unspoiled beaches**.

Jekyll Island Historic District★★

Various tours depart from Jekyll Island Museum (100 Stable Rd.). 912-635-4036. www.jekyllisland. com. The 90-minute tram tour (call or check online for times) allows access to two cottages; $16.

The Queen Anne-style **Jekyll Island Club**, with its signature turret, has been restored as a resort hotel *(371 Riverview Dr.; see Must Stay),* along with the members' former cottages and outbuildings. Even the shops occupy historic structures: a bookstore fills what was once the infirmary; and the former powerhouse has been restored to house the **Georgia Sea Turtle Center** *(214 Stable Rd.; 912-635-4444; www.georgiasea-turtlecenter.org),* a rehabilitation

Cottages – Facing the Intracoastal Waterway amid moss-draped oaks, 15 cottages were built by club members beginning in 1887. At that time, decades before a bridge linked Jekyll Island to the mainland, members arrived for the "club season" (January through March) via steamship or private yacht.

♦ **Goodyear Cottage**, built for lumber baron Frank Goodyear in 1906, is open to the public on a regular basis *(Mon–Fri noon–4pm; weekends 10am–4pm).* It houses the Jekyll Island Art Association, a gift shop and free monthly art exhibit.

♦ With 20 rooms and 13 baths, Italian Renaissance **Crane Cottage** (1917) was the

©M.Linda Lee/Michelin
Goodyear Cottage

GEORGIA'S GOLDEN ISLES

St. Simons Trolley

*Departs from 117 Mallery Street in Pier Village year-round daily 11am. 912-638-8954. www.stsimonstours.com. $22 adults; $10 children (ages 4–12).*This 90-minute narrated tram tour takes you all around St. Simons; along the way you'll learn the island's historical highlights.

grandest on the island; Crane and Cherokee (1904) cottages have both been restored as additions to the hotel.

Faith Chapel – Constructed in 1904, this little wooden chapel once held services for the members of the Jekyll Island Club. Stop in to see the chapel's striking stained-glass windows, designed by Louis Comfort Tiffany and D. Maitland Armstrong.

St. Simons Island★

77mi south of Savannah. From I-95, take Exit 9 and follow US-17 South to St. Simons Causeway.

Largest of the Golden Isles, St. Simons is known for its beautiful beaches as well as its colorful history. Beginning in 1736, when James Oglethorpe built Fort Frederica here, the English and Spanish struggled for control of the island. Oglethorpe attempted unsuccessfully to capture the Spanish fort in St. Augustine, Florida, in 1740; the Spanish counterattack came two years later. During the **Battle of Bloody Marsh** in 1742, Oglethorpe and his forces soundly defeated the Spaniards, who retreated back to Florida (a small monument off Demere Road marks the battle site). In the years before the Civil War, St. Simons was blanketed with cotton plantations, known for their high-quality Sea Island cotton. Now resort hotels and golf clubs cover much of the former plantation land.

Village – The tiny village at the island's southern tip centers on Mallory Street *(off Kings Way/Ocean Blvd.)*. This is where you'll find shops and restaurants, as well as the public pier *(end of Mallory St.)*.

Fort Frederica National Monument★ – *At the end of Frederica Rd. 912-638-3639.*

Marsh creek on St. Simons Island

©Georgia Department of Economic Development

MUST SEE

Little St. Simons

Accessible only by boat from the Hampton River Club Marina on the north end of St. Simons Island. Call for reservations. 912-638-7472 or 888-733-5774. www.littlestsimonsisland.com.

Ten thousand acres of natural beauty and solitude are what you'll find at private Little St. Simons Island. No crowds disturb this tranquil spot; only 30 people at a time are permitted on the island. Purchased for its cedar trees in the early 1900s by pencil manufacturer Philip Berolzheimer, Little St. Simons now offers accommodations in six cottages, including the elegantly appointed three-bedroom Helen House. Spend your days here canoeing the winding tidal creeks, biking the 15 miles of trails, or strolling the 7 miles of deserted beach.

www.nps.gov/fofr. Grounds open year-round daily 8am–5pm. Closed Dec 25. $3 adults, free for children ages 15 and under. James Oglethorpe and his soldiers built Fort Frederica in 1736 as Georgia's first military outpost. Today the ruins of the square fort and its earthen ramparts stand on a bend in the Frederica River.

St. Simons Lighthouse – *101 Twelfth St. 912-638-4666. www.saintsimonslighthouse.org. Open year-round Mon–Sat 10am–5pm, Sun 1:30pm–5pm. Closed Jan 1, Thanksgiving Day & Dec 24–25. $10.* Icon of the island, this 104-foot-tall working lighthouse stands near the pier, where it has guided sailors since 1872. Climb the 129 steps to the top for a great view of the Golden Isles. You'll find artifacts from the area's maritime past on exhibit in the **Museum of Coastal History** *(closed noon–1pm).*

Sea Island

Accessible via Sea Island Dr. from St. Simons Island.

Ohio automobile magnate Howard Coffin had a vision as he looked out across the undeveloped marshland of Sea Island in 1923. In his mind's eye, he imagined a resort and beachfront homes on the land that once held cotton plantations. Coffin's dream is a reality today; Sea Island, with its residential cottage community, is synonymous with **The Cloister**, a world-class resort *(entrance off Sea Island Dr.; see Must Stay)* that occupies part of the island.

Cumberland Island National Seashore★★

10mi southeast of Brunswick, via I-95 South. Take Exit 2 off I-95 and turn left on Rte. 40; follow Rte. 40 east 9mi to St. Marys, GA. Accessible by ferry only from downtown St. Marys (reservations required; see sidebar p 158). 912-882-4335 www.nps.gov/cuis.

Haven for wild horses, sea turtles, alligators, armadillos and a host of shorebirds, Cumberland Island National Seashore sprawls over 17.5 miles of saltwater marshes, maritime forests and lonely beaches. The largest and least developed of Georgia's barrier islands lies across Cumberland Sound from St. Marys, Georgia. Several cotton plantations operated on the island before Thomas Carnegie (brother of Pittsburgh industrialist Andrew Carnegie) and his wife, Lucy,

Sand dunes and beach on Cumberland Island

©Georgia Department of Economic Development

purchased 4,000 acres here in 1881. The secluded estate they constructed was used for hunting and for entertaining guests. Carnegie descendants owned the land until 1972, when they donated most of their holdings to the National Park Service.

On the Island

Plum Orchard – *Visit by guided tour only. 912-882-4335*. Georgian Revival-style Plum Orchard was built in 1898 for Thomas Carnegie's son, George, and his wife. Imagine the lavish lifestyle that the Carnegies enjoyed as you tour its partly furnished rooms.

Dungeness – The eerie ruins of the mansion Thomas and Lucy

Carnegie built in 1884 now rise amid the island foliage.

Greyfield Inn – Another former Carnegie mansion, the rambling home built in 1900 for Margaret Ricketson, daughter of Thomas and Lucy Carnegie, now operates as an upscale inn *(see Must Stay)*.

Plum Orchard

©Georgia Department of Economic Development

The Scoop on Cumberland Island

Getting to Cumberland Island – Stop first on the mainland at Mainland Visitor Center *(107 St. Marys St.; 912-882-4336; open year-round daily 8:15am–4:30pm; closed Dec 25)*. Ferries leave from 107 W. St. Marys Street *(912-882-4335; www.stmaryswelcome.com; $20 adults, $14 children; reservations suggested)*. Day-use fee to visit the island is $4/person. No supplies are available on the island.

Camping – Reservations *(912-882-4335)* are required for camping on the island, limited to 7 days at both sites. The **backcountry** sites *($2/person/night)* have no facilities; water should be treated. No campfires are permitted. Sea Camp Beach campground *($4/person/night)* has restrooms, cold showers and drinking water. Each campsite has a grill, fire ring, food cage and picnic table.

HOTELS & RESTAURANTS

The following pages feature descriptions of hotels and restaurants selected by Michelin and categorized by price for the Charleston Area, the Grand Strand, the Lowcountry Coast and the Georgia Coast.

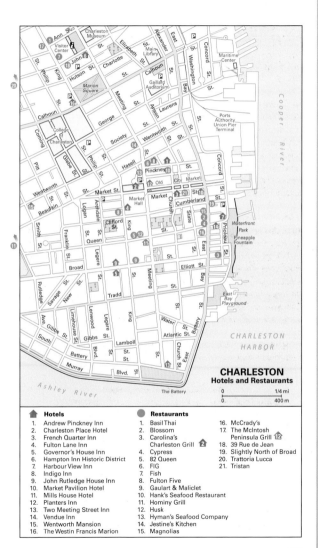

CHARLESTON
Hotels and Restaurants

| 0 | | 1/4 mi |
| 0 | | 400 m |

Hotels
1. Andrew Pinckney Inn
2. Charleston Place Hotel
3. French Quarter Inn
4. Fulton Lane Inn
5. Governor's House Inn
6. Hampton Inn Historic District
7. Harbour View Inn
8. Indigo Inn
9. John Rutledge House Inn
10. Market Pavilion Hotel
11. Mills House Hotel
12. Planters Inn
13. Two Meeting Street Inn
14. Vendue Inn
15. Wentworth Mansion
16. The Westin Francis Marion

Restaurants
1. Basil Thai
2. Blossom
3. Carolina's
    Charleston Grill
4. Cypress
5. 82 Queen
6. FIG
7. Fish
8. Fulton Five
9. Gaulart & Maliclet
10. Hank's Seafood Restaurant
11. Hominy Grill
12. Husk
13. Hyman's Seafood Company
14. Jestine's Kitchen
15. Magnolias
16. McCrady's
17. The McIntosh
    Peninsula Grill
18. 39 Rue de Jean
19. Slightly North of Broad
20. Trattoria Lucca
21. Tristan

RESTAURANTS

The venues listed below were selected for their ambience, location and/or value for money. Rates indicate the average cost of an appetizer, an entrée and a dessert for one person (not including tax, gratuity or beverages). Most restaurants are open daily (except where noted) and accept major credit cards. Call for information regarding reservations, dress code and opening hours.

Luxury	**$$$$**	over $50	*Moderate*	**$$**	$15-$30
Expensive	**$$$**	$30-$50	*Inexpensive*	**$**	under $15

Charleston Area

Properties are located in Charleston unless otherwise noted.

Luxury

Charleston Grill

$$$$ **Contemporary**
In Charleston Place Hotel.
205 Meeting St. (main entrance off Hassell St.). Dinner only. 843-577-4522. www.charlestongrill.com.
Chef Michelle Weaver holds sway at Charleston Place Hotel, where her cuisine wins raves. In the dining room, cream-colored leather seating and mahogany-paneled walls set the stage for a meal to remember. Dishes are divided into four categories. "Pure" spotlights simple preparations with pristine flavors, while "Lush" dishes take cues from classic French technique. "Cosmopolitan" fare shows off Weaver's penchant for Thai flavors; and the "Southern" menu highlights the likes of Country Captain catfish stew.

🍖 Husk

$$$$ **Southern**
76 Queen St. 843-577-2500.
www.huskrestaurant.com.
James Beard Award winner Chef Sean Brock's newest restaurant (he also owns McCrady's) pays homage to the South in ingredients sourced from below the Mason-Dixon Line. The casually elegant dining room, which occupies a structure that dates to 1893, echoes the Lowcountry in its soft colors and natural design elements. Brock works magic with top-quality ingredients from White Oak Pastures beef to Giddy Goat Cheese, and his cuisine sings with layers of carefully constructed flavors. Don't pass up a skillet of the Benton's bacon cornbread.

McCrady's

$$$$ **Contemporary**
2 Unity Alley. 843-577-0025.
www.mccradysrestaurant.com.
Tucked off East Bay Street, Charleston's first tavern (1778) retains its

McCrady's

©McCrady's

Old English style with timbered ceilings, wrought-iron light fixtures, arched doorways and original brick walls. Executive Chef Sean Brock sets his sights on South Carolina products in creations such as grilled cobia with country ham broth and collards, and Ace Basin chicken baked in hay. Much of the produce served here comes from the restaurant's "kitchen garden" on nearby Wadamalaw Island.

Peninsula Grill

$$$$ **Contemporary**
112 N. Market St., at the Planters Inn. Dinner only. 843-723-0700. www.peninsulagrill.com.
Opened in 1987, the Peninsula Grill keeps them coming back with good food and matching service in a romantic dining room, accented with velvet-covered walls and warm-toned cypress woodwork. A crisp, cold wedge of iceberg lettuce topped with buttermilk dressing makes a good prelude to peach-glazed jumbo shrimp with Lowcountry hoppin' John and pan-roasted Carolina rainbow trout with Geechie Boy tomato confit. The signature dessert is the impossibly high—seven layers' worth—and scrumptious coconut cake. If you don't have room to try it after dinner, don't despair; the restaurant will be glad to ship one to you.

Woodlands Resort & Inn

$$$$ **Contemporary**
125 Parsons Rd., Summerville. Dinner Mon–Sat. Lunch Fri & Sat. Closed Sun. 843-875-2600. www.woodlandsinn.com.
Woodlands is a dining destination and a luxury resort rolled into one. Book yourself into one of the 19 sumptuous rooms (**$$$$–$$$$$**)

so you don't have to drive home after a fabulous feast. Jackets are required in the elegant dining room, where the walls and ceiling glimmer under gold glazes, and à la carte tasting menus will wow your taste buds with truffled cauliflower soup and a Wagyu beef ribeye with foie gras butter.

Expensive

Atlanticville

$$$ **Contemporary**
2063 Middle St., Sullivans Island. Dinner & Sun brunch. 843-883-9452. www.atlanticville.net.
Located along Sullivan's Island's little restaurant strip, Atlanticville feels like your aunt's old beach house, with its paneled walls, Victorian décor and white tablecloths. The food, on the other hand, puts a Lowcountry spin on contemporary cuisine, like whole fried flounder with red rice and tomato-stewed collards, and roasted salmon and shrimp over a bed of caramelized-onion grits.

Blossom

$$$ **Lowcountry**
171 E. Bay St. 843-722-9200. www.magnolias-blossom-cypress.com.
Magnolias' casual little sister, this Charleston staple remains a lively spot that specializes in Lowcountry fare, with a focus on seafood. Grilled yellowfin tuna, lump crab cakes and buttermilk fried shrimp are just a few of the tempting selections. Fans always appreciate the crispy wood-oven pizzas and house-made pastas. In nice weather, grab a seat outside on the patio.

RESTAURANTS

The Boathouse at Breach Inlet

$$$ **Seafood**

101 Palm Blvd., Isle of Palms. Dinner & Sun brunch. 843-886-8000. www.boathouserestaurants.com.

There's always a crowd at this waterfront seafood place. "Simply fresh seafood" is the mantra here, where fresh fish such as yellowfin tuna, black grouper and local snapper are grilled and come with your choice of sauces and sides. The signature lobster and crab cake (three petit coldwater lobster tails and one of the Boathouse's jumbo lump crab cakes) also comes in variations with filet mignon. Come in time to watch the sunset over Breach Inlet from your table or from the rooftop Crow Bar.

Carolina's

$$$ **Lowcountry**

10 Exchange St. Dinner & Sun brunch. 843-724-3800. www.carolinasrestaurant.com.

Regional seafood stars in this casual-chic dining room, with pecky cypress beams, antique mirrors and custom lighting and tiles. In this 18C structure, appetizers like house-made bucatini pasta and entrées such as pan-sautéed flounder with country ham enhance the Lowcountry's culinary heritage—and are guaranteed to please your palate.

Cypress

$$$ **Contemporary**

167 E. Bay St. Dinner only. 843-727-0111. www.magnolias-blossom-cypress.com.

Occupying an 1834 building with exposed brick walls and high ceilings, this sleek eatery packs in locals and visitors for regional cuisine by renowned chef Craig Deihl. Complement crisp wasabi tuna, hickory-grilled filet of beef or smoked-salmon Wellington with your choice of wine from the 4,500 bottles lining the three-story wine wall. Tableside preparations for two—Chateaubriand and herb-rubbed rack of lamb—are one of the reasons Cypress has been awarded the local vote for "Most Romantic Restaurant." Save room for the coconut panna cotta.

82 Queen

$$$ **Lowcountry**

82 Queen St. Lunch Mon–Fri. Dinner daily. 843-723-7591. www.82queen.com.

Crab cakes, 82 Queen

©82 Queen

Charleston's special-occasion restaurant since 1982 sits in the heart of the Historic District. Its two connecting 19C row houses contain 11 romantic dining rooms. In nice weather, ask for a table in the shady courtyard. Award-winning she-crab soup, pan-fried lump crab cakes, grilled barbecue shrimp and grits, and bourbon pecan pie highlight the Low-country cuisine at 82 Queen.

FIG

$$$ **Contemporary**

232 Meeting St., at Hassell St. Dinner only. Closed Sun. 843-805-5900. www.eatatfig.com.

MUST EAT

Food is good at this Charleston favorite—and that's coincidentally what FIG's name is an acronym for. In the casual, understated dining room, seasonal fare by James Beard Award-winning chef Mike Lata may include softshell crabs Grenebloise and Strube Ranch Wagyu bistro steak, while the fish stew in cocotte—in an aromatic saffron-scented broth—has been a menu fixture since day one. Take your pick of sides for the table from the likes of Anson Mills farro piccolo and tender sautéed kale.

Fish

$$$ **Seafood**
442 King St. No lunch Sat.
Closed Sun. 843-722-3474.
www.fishrestaurant.net.

An 1837 single house is the setting for sensational seafood in this upper King Street restaurant. Recycled materials were used to update the interior, while the menu exhibits a French-Asian flair. For dinner, that might mean a dim sum of crab rangoon, spicy tuna and frog leg wonton, or large plates such as pan-seared scallops with coconut rice, and tempura chicken with pad Thai noodles. If you prefer simpler preparations, order the "naked" fish of the day.

Fulton Five

$$$ **Italian**
5 Fulton St. Dinner only.
Closed Sun. 843-853-5555.
www.fultonfive.net.

Sage-green walls and crisp white tablecloths greet visitors to this cozy dining room, where Northern Italian fare rules. The seasonally changing menu might feature chocolate and espresso-rubbed beef filet over whipped potatoes, or a grilled veal T-bone with roasted zucchini. The *pesce del giorno* (fish of the day) nets a different preparation daily. Whatever is on the menu when you visit, one thing is for sure: high-quality imported ingredients—prosciutto, olive oil, fine cheeses and aged balsamic vinegar—make a meal at Fulton Five one to remember.

Hank's Seafood Restaurant

$$$ **Seafood**
10 Hayne St. (at Church St.).
Dinner only. 843-723-3474.
www.hanksseafoodrestaurant.com.

Hank's classy dining room has

Fish

©Andrew Cebulka

Fulton Five

©Christine Mahoney/Michelin

risen to local stardom since it appeared on the scene in 1999. After you whet your appetite with award-winning she-crab soup, crispy rock shrimp and calamari, or an oyster sampler from the raw bar, you'll have to choose between such tantalizing house specialties as roast grouper with a shrimp basil butter *jus*, and a standout version of shrimp and grits—local shrimp, andouille sausage and stewed tomatoes atop creamy stone-ground grits.

Magnolias

$$$ Southern
185 E. Bay St. 843-577-7771.
www.magnolias-blossom-cypress.com.
Chef Donald Barickman classifies his menu here as "Uptown/Down South." That roughly translates to highbrow Southern food served in an upscale atmosphere, highlighted by wrought-iron elements and original artwork. Start with a bowl of the acclaimed blue-crab bisque, and move on to Carolina Carpetbagger filet with fried oysters, or parmesan-crusted flounder over jasmine rice. You won't find swordfish on the menu here, since Magnolias' staff supports the efforts being made to conserve all billfish species.

The McIntosh

$$$ Contemporary
479-B King St. Dinner & Sun.
brunch. 843-789-4299.
www.themcintoshcharleston.com.
This new addition to the ever-changing Charleston dining scene fashions a casual, industrial-chic lair with its exposed ductwork and contemporary light fixtures. In the open kitchen at the back, chef/partner Jeremiah Bacon changes his menu daily to reflect the best of the season. That might mean starters of house-made wild ramp cavatelli or ricotta gnudi with broccoli rabe pesto, while entrées tempt with a grilled deckle steak with celeriac purée and sautéed American red snapper with brown butter crumble. Though sides go off the grid in bone-marrow bread pudding and maple-glazed roasted turnips, the pecorino truffle fries always win raves.

Red Drum Gastropub

$$$ Southwestern
803 Coleman Blvd., Mt. Pleasant.
Dinner only & Sun brunch.
Closed Mon. 843-849-0313.
www.reddrumrestaurant.com.
It's well worth a trip across the

Shellfish over grits, Magnolias

©Magnolias

Cooper River Bridge for a meal at the Red Drum in Mt. Pleasant. Here, chef/owner Ben Berryhill brings his expertise all the way from Café Annie in Houston, Texas. Berryhill uses Southwestern accents to spike the likes of wood-grilled Scottish salmon with a sweet corn pudding tamale. Appetizers offer a taste of the American Southwest with beet empanadas and the ceviche of the day. The bar attracts a lively crowd at happy hour, while the brick patio, framed by wrought-iron gates, makes a great alfresco spot for a drink or a meal when the area's notorious humidity permits.

Slightly North of Broad
©Maverick Southern Kitchens

Rosebank Farms Café

$$$ **Southern**

Bohicket Marina Village, John's Island. 843-768-1807. www.rosebankfarmscafe.com.

A perfect place for a casual lunch or dinner, this little cafe facing the marina between Kiawah and Seabrook islands presents fresh seafood, meat and local produce prepared with Southern attitude. Try any of the Blue Plate Specials for lunch, and don't forget to order a piece of Key lime pie for dessert. In true Southern style, the revamped dinner menu has a special section devoted to grits. Among the entrées, a Charleston-style paella highlights local seafood, and honey buttermilk fried chicken comes with collard greens and Yukon Gold mashed potatoes.

Slightly North of Broad

$$$ **Lowcountry**

192 E. Bay St. No lunch Sat–Sun. 843-723-3424. www.maverick southernkitchens.com.

Humor resides within the walls of

this 19C brick warehouse, whose current tenant takes its tongue-in-cheek name from its less-than-coveted location (historically, the best place to live in Charleston was south of Broad Street). Ironically, it's no mistake that the restaurant's acronym spells "SNOB." Chef Frank Lee, a South Carolina native, may trade his toque for a baseball cap, but he doesn't skimp on flavor. Songs of the South ring out in an apple and cornbread-stuffed Carolina quail breast, and the Maverick shrimp and grits—made with local shrimp, house-made sausage and country ham.

Trattoria Lucca

$$$ **Italian**

41 Bogard St. Dinner only. Closed Sun 843-577-7771. www.luccacharleston.com.

Off the beaten track in Charleston's Elliotsborough neighborhood, this cozy trattoria showcases the cooking of Chef Ken Vedrinksi. Handmade pastas (think ricotta cavatelli with local flounder and fusili bucati with house-made wild boar sausage) are always a hit. But don't pass up *piatti*—such as pancetta-wrapped grouper with first of season local tomato bread salad—that combine local ingredients with Italian flair. Come

165

Monday nights for the family-style supper: four set courses served at a communal table for $38/person.

Tristan
$$$ **Contemporary**
55 Market St. 843-534-2155.
www.tristandining.com.
Tristan bills its creative cuisine as "globally influenced, bold American." Each dish is served with style in an Art Deco-inspired, 100-seat dining room. Banquettes and chairs upholstered in blue and silver flank tables arranged around the open kitchen, where Chef Nate Whiting prepares such enticing dishes as seared New England scallops with crispy pepperoni, and beef loin cooked sous vide. The impressive wine list approaches 500 bottles, with two dozen wines by the glass. Can't decide? Let Tristan's sommelier design pairings for you.

Moderate

Basil Thai
$$ **Thai**
460 King St. Dinner daily.
Lunch Mon–Fri. 843-724-3490.
www.eatatbasil.com.
If it's Thai food you crave, head for Basil, located on upper King Street at Ann Street. Be prepared to wait in line, though, since the popular eatery doesn't accept reservations. Even so, it's worth a wait for spicy green, red or masaman curries and other authentic dishes.
Specialties include Pad Thai and basil duck—a deep-fried, boneless half-duck topped with vegetables and basil sauce. Entrées are available with your choice of beef, chicken, pork, shrimp or tofu.

Gaulart & Maliclet
$$ **French**
98 Broad St. Closed Sun. 843-577-9797. www.fastandfrench.org.
"Fast and French" is the motto of this small eatery, a favorite with Charleston's business lunchers. Pull up a stool at the communal counter and make a new friend; lunch specials include a glass of wine to promote the convivial atmosphere. For dinner, entrées range from seafood Normandy to beef Bordelaise to chicken Provençal. There are "ethnic specials" on Friday and Saturday, and a selection of fondues on Thursday.

Gaulart & Maliclet

©Susan Pittard/Gaulart & Maliclet

Hominy Grill
$$ **Southern**
207 Rutledge Ave. Breakfast, lunch & dinner Mon–Fri. Brunch Sat & Sun. 843-937-0930.
www.hominygrill.com.
The staff at Hominy Grill believes you are what you eat. So they get their produce from area farms, their fish from local waters and their grits from a water-powered mill in North Carolina, near where chef Robert Stehling grew up. Hominy Grill is located in an 1897

Charleston single house about 12 blocks outside the Historic District—but it's worth the detour for the likes of sesame-crusted farm-raised catfish and fried chicken with ham gravy and fluffy biscuits. Try a piece of the the fresh fruit pie or the creamy chocolate pudding for dessert.

Hyman's Seafood Company
$$ Seafood
215 Meeting St. 843-723-6000.
www.hymanseafood.com.
It seems there's always a line out the door at this popular seafood spot. And it's easy to see why—Hyman's orders fresh seafood daily and offers at least 15 choices on its menu board. Although they'll prepare your fish any way you like it (broiled, steamed, blackened, or even with Caribbean jerk seasoning), fried is clearly the preferred method.
Can't decide? Go for one of the combo platters and make sure you include the crispy flounder, a house specialty. And save room for the Key lime pie.

Jestine's Kitchen
$$ Southern
251 Meeting St., at the corner of Wentworth St. Closed Mon.
843-722-7224.
Looking for Southern soul food? You'll find it at this Charleston institution, named for Jestine Matthews, who cared for the family of the restaurant's founder and lived to be 112 years old. Wash down fried chicken, fried green tomatoes, meatloaf or pecan-crusted whiting with Jestine's" table wine"—real Southern sweet tea. For dessert, the Coca-Cola cake is the hands-down favorite.

39 Rue de Jean
$$-$$$ French
39 John St. 843-722-8881.
www.39ruedejean.com.
With its tin ceiling, exposed-brick walls and zinc bar, this bustling brasserie looks—and tastes—French. Bistro classics such as *steak frites* and *salade Niçoise* share menu space with a selection of sushi—an unexpected addition. The more traditional chef's *plats*

39 Rue de Jean
©39 Rue de Jean

du jour include braised short ribs, bouillabaisse and coq au vin. Steamed mussels *(moules)*, a signature dish here, come prepared six different ways; marinière, bacon bleu cheese, pistou, curry, aïoli, and vegetable cream.

The Grand Strand

Expensive

Bistro 217

$$$ **Contemporary**
10707 Ocean Hwy., Pawleys Island. 843-235-8217. www.bistro217.com.
Dine inside or out at this casual fine-dining restaurant, located off busy Highway 17 within a small strip of upscale shops. Pastel colors and zebra-striped banquettes adorn the dining room, while the spacious covered courtyard sports wrought-iron furniture and ceiling fans. For lunch try the tasty fish tacos. There's a children's menu available at lunchtime. For dinner, start off with an appetizer such as the fried green tomatoes and oysters. Then move on to the 217 Eggplant Treasure Chest, made with fried eggplant and local shrimp, scallops and grouper.

Bistro 217 fish tacos
©Gwen Cannon/Michelin

Collector's Cafe

$$$ **Mediterranean**
7726 N. Kings Hwy., Myrtle Beach. Closed Sun. 843-449-9370. www.collectorscafeandgallery.com.
Is it an art gallery or a restaurant? You be the judge. In fact, you can buy art and eat at Collector's Cafe, where hand-painting decorates tables, chairs and tiles, and original artwork blankets the walls. As for the food, pan-sautéed scallop cakes are served with tomato-scallion-garlic butter sauce; veal medallions are grilled and paired with shrimp macaroni and cheese; and yellowfin tuna is grilled rare and laid over an Oriental couscous salad. Between the ambience and the cuisine, Collector's Cafe is a masterpiece.

Frank's and Frank's Outback

$$$ **Contemporary**
10434 Ocean Hwy., Pawleys Island. Dinner only. Closed Sun. 843-237-3030. www.franksandoutback.com.
Named for the owner of a supermarket that once occupied this site, Frank's has been a local favorite since it opened in 1988. Seafood shines in cornmeal-crusted grouper over grits, Carolina white shrimp with cannellini beans, and the fresh fish of the day. Meanwhile, meat lovers will find much to satisfy them in the chophouse steak menu.
For outdoor dining, try **Frank's Outback ($$–$$$)**, where you can enjoy wood-fired pizzas or heartier entrées under tall oaks. In crisp weather, there are infrared heaters and an outdoor fireplace to warm you; all year-round, live music plays on weekends.

MUST EAT

Frank's Restaurant

©Gwen Cannon/Michelin

Lee's Inlet Kitchen

$$$ **Seafood**

4460 Business 17, Murrells Inlet. Dinner only. Closed Sun. 843-651-2881. www.leesinletkitchen.com.

Prices have hiked up a bit since Pearl and Eford Lee started their Murrells Inlet eatery in 1948. At that time, the seafood platter cost $1.50; now it's $25.95, but it still satisfies seafood lovers with a heaping portion of flounder, fantail shrimp, oysters, scallops and deviled crab (broiled or fried). And if that's not enough, your dinner comes with a salad, a choice of potato or vegetable, and fried hush puppies—a Southern favorite.

The Library

$$$ **Continental**

1212 N. Kings Hwy., Myrtle Beach. Dinner only. Closed Sun. 843-448-4527. www.thelibraryrestaurantsc.com.

With its tuxedoed waitstaff and traditional tableside preparations (think Caesar salad, steak Diane, sweetbreads and flambé desserts—sure to impress a date), The Library has been the Grand Stand's special-occasion restaurant

The Library

©The Library Restaurant

since it opened its doors in 1974. Rack of lamb, duck à l'orange, chicken with artichokes, and twin lobster tails are just a few of the selections that will tempt your tastebuds here.

Phillips Seafood

$$$ **Seafood**

1807 21st Ave. N., Myrtle Beach. Dinner only. Call for off-season hours. 843-626-2722. www.phillipsseafood.com.

Born as Phillips Crab House in Ocean City, Maryland, in 1956, this venerable seafood chain opened its Myrtle Beach outpost in 2003. Crab is king here, even though the menu lists a tempting selection of fried, broiled and grilled fish as well. The signature dish is the premium crab cakes, made with jumbo lump crab meat, barely held together with mayonnaise and Phillips special seasonings—and it's worth the premium price. Other specialties include baked scallops stuffed with crab imperial, and the broiled seafood platter—a hearty combo that includes the catch of the day, jumbo shrimp, scallops and a crab cake.

Sea Captain's House
$$$ **Seafood**
3002 N. Ocean Blvd.,
Myrtle Beach. 843-448-8082.
www.seacaptains.com.
This nautical-themed restaurant overlooking the Atlantic has a long history as a private beach cottage, and later as a guest house. Happily, it still welcomes patrons who enjoy good food with an ocean view. Reasonably priced dinner entrées include crab cakes, broiled or fried shrimp, ribeye steak, grilled pork chops, and the fresh catch of the day. The special children's menu makes this a good restaurant for families.

Moderate

Hard Rock Cafe
$$ **American**
Broadway at the Beach, US-17 at 21st Ave. N., Myrtle Beach. 843-946-0007. www.hardrockcafe.com.
You can't miss the Hard Rock Cafe at Myrtle Beach—it's shaped like an Egyptian pyramid, complete with sphinxes guarding the entrance. Inside, it's all American, though, from the burgers and barbecue to the blaring old-time rock 'n roll. The décor is rock memorabilia: guitars once played by greats like the Allman Brothers, Jimi Hendrix and Jerry Garcia line the walls, along with tons of gold and platinum records honoring hits by everyone from the Beatles to the Osmonds. Sure it's touristy, but the kids will want to go.

Island Cafe and Deli
$$ **Seafood**
10683 Ocean Hwy., Pawleys Island. 843-237-9527.
www.islandcafeanddeli.com.
Most customers like to eat outside under the awning, despite the constant traffic on US-17. Huge fans here will keep you cool in summer. Monday night is shrimp night; you'll get a pound of the Atlantic crustaceans, cooked any way you like. On Tuesday and Wednesday the special is Maine lobster *(reservations advised).* Otherwise, start with the oysters and fried green tomatoes in a bleu cheese and bacon cream sauce, and move on to blackened grouper over cheesy grits and vegetables with mustard bacon butter. End your meal with a little toe tapping to live music every Monday at dinnertime in summer.

Island Cafe and Deli

©Gwen Cannon/Michelin

Croissants Bistro and Bakery
$-$$ **International**
3751 Grissom Pkwy., Myrtle Beach. 843-448-2253. www.croissants.net.
Croissants makes a good place for that pre-golf breakfast, a noon break from the sun, late afternoon tapas *(after 4pm)* or dinner. For lunch, try the quiche of the day, the pimento cheese and artichoke melt, or a Monte Cristo sandwich. Then sally up to the pastry case and drool over the mouthwatering array of cakes and tortes.

Wedding cake, Croissants Bistro and Bakery

©Croissants Bistro & Bakery/Carmen Ash Photography

Eggs Up Grill
$ **American**
13088 Ocean Hwy., Pawleys Island. Breakfast & lunch only. 843-237-7313. www.eggsupgrill.com.
Eggs any way—that's what you'll get at this popular local breakfast haunt. Besides the basics, there are corned-beef hash and eggs, eggs Benedict, pancakes and eggs, and steak and eggs. Or you can customize your own three-egg omelet with a choice of fillings. If you're not watching your carb intake, go for a Belgian waffle or the cinnamon-raisin French toast. Fresh sandwiches and burgers round out the menu at lunchtime.

Lowcountry Coast

Expensive

Michael Anthony's Cucina Italiana
$$$ **Italian**
37 New Orleans Rd., in Orleans Plaza, Hilton Head Island. Dinner only. Closed Sun. 843-785-6272. www.michael-anthonys.com.
Authentic Italian food comes to Hilton Head at this popular restaurant, whose sleek dining room is done in warm wood tones and soft colors. Savor the likes of homemade potato gnocchi with fresh tomatoes and basil; filet mignon topped with mushrooms and Gorgonzola in a Barolo wine sauce; and veal alla Zingara (scaloppini of veal sautéed with white wine, pancetta, olives, mushrooms and cherry peppers in a fresh tomato sauce). For dessert, the signature tiramisu classico (ladyfingers soaked in espresso and rum, and layered with mascarpone mousse and cocoa) can't be beat.

Old Oyster Factory
$$$ **Seafood**
101 Marshland Rd., Hilton Head Island (1mi off Mathews Dr.). Dinner only. 843-681-6040. www.oldoysterfactory.com.
As you'd expect from a restaurant built on the site of one of Hilton Head's original oyster canneries, oysters come fresh from the local waters here. The island landmark features an open dining room with lots of floor-to-ceiling windows for views of Broad Creek and the surrounding marshland on three sides. Big appetites should go for the seafood medley, a platter piled high with fresh shrimp,

RESTAURANTS

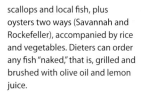

scallops and local fish, plus oysters two ways (Savannah and Rockefeller), accompanied by rice and vegetables. Dieters can order any fish "naked," that is, grilled and brushed with olive oil and lemon juice.

Plums Waterfront Restaurant
$$$ **Seafood**
904 Bay St., Beaufort.
843-525-1946.
www.plumsrestaurant.com
Plums' lively bistro atmosphere, with folk art adorning the walls, has been drawing local crowds since 1986. Try the whole fried flounder with sweet-potato chips, or go for the lighter shrimp farfalle in white wine garlic sauce. Carolina crab cakes, made with succulent lump crab meat, are another good bet. Come listen to live music on Thursday, Friday and Saturday nights.

Red Fish
$$$ **Seafood**
8 Archer Rd., Hilton Head Island.
No lunch Sun. 843-686-3388.
www.redfishofhiltonhead.com.
On your way into Red Fish, stop at the restaurant's wine shop and pick up a bottle to complement the Cuban- and Caribbean-inspired fare, which ranges from Dominican braised pork in coconut milk, cilantro and chilies with fried bananas, white rice and Cuban black beans to spicy Latin ribs with guava-orange barbecue sauce. For dessert, try the caramelized bread pudding or a dessert martini for two. The real deal here is the early dining menu *(served from 5pm–5:45pm)*: two courses plus a beverage for just $14.95.

Saltus River Grill
$$$ **Seafood**
802 Bay St., Beaufort.
Dinner only. 843-379-3474.
www.saltusrivergrill.com.

Saltus River Grill
©Saltus River Grill

This sophisticated spot overlooking the Intracoastal Waterway occupies the site of an 18C shipyard; decorating the walls, photographs mounted on sail canvas recall the building's past. You can't go wrong with entrées like Sea Island shrimp and creamy stone-ground grits, skillet-browned crab cakes, or barbecue-glazed salmon belly. There's also a full sushi menu and an amazing list of oysters—the restaurant offers more than 60 types, from both the Atlantic and the Pacific.

Moderate

Smokehouse
$$ **American**
34 Palmetto Bay Rd., Hilton Head Island. 843-842-4227.
www.smokehousehi.com.
At this local favorite, barbecue fans can chow down on house specialties like slow-smoked, hand-pulled pork, a honey-glazed smoked chicken, or a rack of ribs

MUST EAT

that are dry-rubbed and smoked over hickory wood. For seafood lovers, there's grilled grouper and local shrimp; most entrées come with a choice of two sides. In nice weather, the outdoor deck is a great spot for an alfresco meal and a frozen daiquiri, but if you'd rather eat inside, the dining room boasts a 30-foot retractable window. And with 15 TVs, both inside and out, you'll never miss that championship game. Live music entertains diners on weekends.

Shrimp Shack
$$ Seafood
1925 Sea Island Pkwy., St. Helena Island. Lunch Mon–Sat; dinner Fri & Sat only. Closed Sun. 843-838-2962.
Locals flock to this ultra-casual waterside eatery 15 minutes downwind of Beaufort, which has graced St. Helena Island for some 20 years. Probably the most popular item on the menu is their shrimp burger, but the crab cakes and flounder sandwiches are not far behind. Forget about that low-carb diet and go for the sweet-potato fries.

Inexpensive

Blackstone's Cafe
$ American
205 Scott St., Beaufort. Breakfast & lunch only. 843-524-4330. www.blackstonescafe.com.
This favorite breakfast and lunchtime gathering place emphasizes local seafood in its regional offerings. It's hard to top Blackstone's shrimp omelet and grits in the morning—stone-ground white and yellow grits are

the house specialty. For midday meals, try the homemade soups. Sandwiches, salads and seafood dishes round out the menu. On a sunny day, you can enjoy the cafe's patio service.

The Georgia Coast

Luxury

Elizabeth on 37th
$$$$ Southern
105 E. 37th St., Savannah. Dinner only. 912-236-5547. www.elizabethon37th.net.
Award-winning chef Elizabeth Terry and her husband, Michael, opened this restaurant in 1981 in a lovely Greek Revival-style mansion built for a wealthy cotton broker in the late 19C. Now executive chef Kelly Yambor continues the restaurant's culinary magic. Sesame- and almond-crusted coastal grouper; spicy Savannah red rice with Georgia shrimp, sausage and okra; and a double-cut Berkshire pork chop with five-cheese macaroni number among the mouthwatering menu choices. Yambor accents her seasonal selections with herbs from the restaurant's garden. A 7-course tasting menu is offered as well. Save room for the Savannah cream cake; it is as rich as it sounds.

Expensive

Latitude 31
$$$ Seafood
370 Riverview Dr., Jekyll Island. Closed Mon. 912-635-3800. www.latitude31jekyllisland.com.
For ideal seafood restaurant settings, you can't beat the historic

RESTAURANTS

Latitude 31

©Brooke Roberts Photography

wharf in Jekyll Island's Landmark District. Located directly across from the Jekyll Island Club Hotel, Latitude 31 serves up just-caught seafood for lunch and dinner. Here, wild Georgia shrimp, jumbo sea scallops and the catch of the day can be grilled, blackened or fried, while a list of entrées adds pan-roasted grouper, fried green tomato parmesan, plus a ribeye filet. Sides like stewed okra, corn and tomatoes highlight local crops. Don't want a full meal? Kick back on the dock and sip a Rum Smash cocktail at the adjacent Rah Bar, where friendly dogs are welcome. Live music entertains diners Thursday through Sunday during the summer.

The Lady & Sons
$$$ **Southern**
102 W. Congress St., Savannah. 912-233-2600. www.ladyandsons.com.
Savannah native Paula Deen was newly divorced and unemployed when she started a catering business in town with her two sons in 1989. The successful endeavor grew into a restaurant, and today The Lady & Sons draws a loyal local following. Located in Savannah's historic City Market, the restaurant focuses on Southern home cooking. The dinner buffet features all-you-can-eat fried chicken, collard greens, green beans, rice and gravy—including salad and dessert—for $17.99. Or order the Savannah crab cakes, chicken pot pie, or steak and tomato pie from the à la carte menu.

Sapphire Grill
$$$ **Contemporary**
110 W. Congress St., Savannah. Dinner only. 912-443-9962. www.sapphiregrill.com.
Fresh and seasonal cuisine is what you'll find at Sapphire Grill, a Savannah hot spot. Chef Christopher Nason hunts down day-boat scallops, local shrimp, heirloom vegetables, and USDA Prime beef for his seasonally changing menu. Sapphire bouillabaisse comes in a

Sapphire Grill

©Sapphire Grill

champagne shellfish bouillon; local black grouper is crusted with nutty benne seeds; and Colorado lamb chops are served on the bone as savory "lollipops." All this bounty is served by an efficient staff against a background of stainless steel, exposed brick walls and original artwork in the chic dining room.

Moderate

🦀 The Crab Shack

$$ **Seafood**
40 Estill Hammock, Tybee Island.
912-786-9857.
www.thecrabshack.com.
A former fish camp, this bare-bones eatery, located 17 miles east of Savannah on tiny Tybee Island, offers the freshest shellfish around. Huge portions of boiled or steamed crabs, shrimp and oysters come with corn on the cob and potatoes. You have to shell them yourself, though, so grab a roll of paper towels, pull up a bench at one of the wooden tables, and crack away. Buckets are provided for the shells.

SeaJay's Waterfront Cafe & Pub

$$ **Seafood**
1 Harbor Rd., Jekyll Island.
912-635-3200. www.seajays.com.
Locals love this little cottage at Jekyll Harbor Marina for its Lowcountry boil buffet—an all-you-can-eat extravaganza of local shrimp, smoked sausage, corn on the cob and new potatoes for just $17.95. And, did we mention cole slaw, rolls and banana pudding for dessert? Dinner platters (shrimp scampi, crab cakes, broiled catch of the day) are served with slaw and a vegetable of the day. SeaJay's original Brunswick Stew, soups, salads and sandwiches are available all day. Request a table outside for great water views.

Inexpensive

Vinnie Van Go-Go's

$ **Italian**
317 W. Bryan St., on Franklin Square, Savannah. No lunch Sat–Sun. 912-233-6394.
www.vinnievangogo.com.
It's not fancy, but locals and visitors alike crowd the indoor and outdoor tables at Vinnie's boisterous City Market location for tasty thin-crust New York-style pizza and generous calzones. Before you go, note that Vinnie's doesn't accept credit cards or reservations.

HOTELS

The properties listed below were selected for their ambience, location and/or value for money. Prices reflect the average cost for a standard double room for two people in high season. High season in Charleston and Savannah is in the spring and fall; rates are considerably lower in summer and winter. High season for the resort islands is in summer. Price ranges quoted do not reflect the South Carolina hotel tax of 12% or the Georgia hotel tax, which varies by county from 3% to 8%.

Luxury	**$$$$$** over $350
Expensive	**$$$$** $250-$350
Moderate	**$$$** $175-$250
Inexpensive	**$$** $100-$175
Budget	**$** Under $100

Charleston Area

Properties listed are in Charleston unless otherwise noted.

Luxury

Charleston Place Hotel
$$$$$ 440 rooms
205 Meeting St. (main entrance off Hassell St.). 843-722-4900 or 888-635-2350.
www.charlestonplace.com.
A 3,000-piece Murano crystal chandelier hangs above the Georgian open-armed staircase in the elegant lobby of the grand dame of Charleston's hostelries, operated by Orient Express Hotels, Inc. Renovated guest rooms have 19C period furnishings, toile and floral patterns, and sumptuous marble baths. Amenities include a spa *(see Spas)*, pool, fitness center, and adjoining shops. Be sure to savor Chef Michelle Weaver's innovative cuisine at the hotel's renowned **Charleston Grill** (*see Must Eat*). Reserve a table for the hotel's famous 🍵**afternoon tea** *(Thu–Sat 1pm–4pm, $32–$38).*

🍵The Sanctuary
$$$$$ 255 rooms
1 Sanctuary Beach Dr., Kiawah Island. 843-768-6000 or 877-683-1234. www.thesanctuary.com.
Designed to resemble a 19C seaside mansion, this luxurious oceanfront hotel is flanked by 150-year-old transplanted live oaks on one side and the Atlantic Ocean on the other. The lobby feels like

Charleston Place Hotel

©Charleston Place Hotel

Boardwalk Inn

©Wild Dunes Resort

someone's lavish living room, with its 25-foot-high ceilings and ocean view. Room décor sports tones of gold and green; spacious marble baths have his-and-hers vanities and deep soaking tubs.

Chill out on the beach or the palm-studded pool deck, or enjoy a treatment at the spa (see Spas). You'll enjoy contemporary cuisine at the formal **Ocean Room ($$$$)**, or Lowcountry fare at clubby **Jasmine Porch ($$$)**.

Wentworth Mansion

$$$$$ 21 rooms
149 Wentworth St. 843-853-1886 or 888-466-1886. www.wentworth mansion.com.

A bit off the beaten track, Wentworth Mansion envelops guests in opulent surroundings— hand-carved marble fireplaces, Tiffany stained-glass windows, rich woodwork—in quarters built for a wealthy cotton merchant in 1886. Roomy chambers have king-size beds, gas fireplaces, hardwood floors and whirlpool tubs. The day begins with a complimentary breakfast buffet served on the airy sunporch. Then relax by the fireplace in the parlor, curl up with a book in the library, or treat

yourself to a session in the spa. Savor the contemporary fare served at the on-site **Circa 1886 ($$$)** restaurant.

Expensive

Boardwalk Inn

$$$$ 93 rooms
Palmetto Dr. at Wild Dunes, Isle of Palms. 843-886-6000 or 877-778-1876. www.wilddunes.com.

If you don't want to rent a place for a whole week at Wild Dunes resort, this inn is a great option. You'll still have access to all the resort's amenities, which include a fitness center, tennis courts, and two award-winning golf courses. When you're not relaxing in your balconied room with its sand and coral palette, you can pedal along the bike paths, swim in the pools, or just lie on the beach.

French Quarter Inn

$$$$ 50 rooms
166 Church St. 843-722-1900 or 866-812-1900. www.fqicharleston.com.

Champagne and ladyfinger cookies greet you at check-in at this inn, located just around the corner from Market Street. At

HOTELS

night, slip into the triple-sheeted European bedding and choose one of seven different selections on the inn's pillow menu. Service is a cut above, and Parisian charm begins in the elegant lobby and continues in rooms outfitted with carved headboards and toile bed throws. For business travelers, suites come complete with a computer, high-speed Internet access, a color printer and fax machine.

Harbour View Inn
$$$$ 52 rooms
2 Vendue Range. 843-853-8439 or 888-853-8439. www.harbourview charleston.com.
Adjacent to Waterfront Park, this family-friendly property overlooks Charleston Harbor. The lobby area, with its island-inspired décor, recalls the days when many of Charleston's residents hailed from the Caribbean. Lowcountry-style guest rooms feature 14-foot ceilings, four-poster bed, wicker furnishings and seagrass rugs. Many rooms have harbor views. Rates include a continental breakfast, evening cookies and milk, and turn-down service.

John Rutledge House Inn
$$$$ 19 rooms
116 Broad St. 843-723-7999 or 866-720-2609. www.johnrutledge houseinn.com.
A rough draft of the Constitution was written in this 1763 house, and resident John Rutledge was one of the 55 men who signed it. Inlaid parquet floors, canopied rice beds, carved plaster moldings, and antiques and period reproductions typify this National Historic Landmark's restoration to its mid-18C appearance. A continental

breakfast and evening wine and sherry are compliments of the house.

Market Pavilion Hotel
$$$$ 70 rooms
225 E. Bay St. 843-723-0500 or 877-440-2250. www.marketpavilion.com.
This luxury property sits on the corner of East Bay and Market streets within the historic district; double-paned windows help screen out the noise. Your room will have its own foyer, mahogany furnishings and elegant window treatments. Sleep in style on Frette linens, with cashmere blankets and down pillows. Italian marble baths come with fluffy towels and robes. **Grill 225 ($$$$)** specializes in chophouse fare, while the rooftop **Pavilion Bar** *(see Musts for Fun)* boasts a great view.

Mills House Hotel
$$$$ 214 rooms
115 Meeting St. 843-577-2400 or 800-874-9600. www.millshouse.com.
This hotel has nearly everything you could ask for in a moderately priced property: an outdoor pool, a courtyard, two bars, the **Barbadoes Room ($$$)** restaurant (try their Sunday brunch), and a Grand Ballroom—and it's all set on Meeting Street, in the heart of the historic district. Well-appointed rooms boast period furnishings and come with nightly turn-down service. On the private-access executive level, the room rate includes a continental breakfast and evening hors d'oeuvres.

MUST STAY

Planters Inn

$$$$ **64 rooms**
112 N. Market St. 843-722-2345
or 800-845-7082.
www.plantersinn.com.

Planters Inn

This Relais & Châteaux property occupies the corner of Market and Meeting streets in the historic district. (Rooms are equipped with a white-noise machine to filter out sounds of nighttime revelry on Market Street.) Lodgings in the original 1844 building are designed in subtle colors with four-poster canopy beds, reproduction pieces and high ceilings. The back building carries on the vintage feel, with 21 rooms overlooking the courtyard's palm trees from a breezy loggia. Sample the contemporary American fare at the inn's **Peninsula Grill** *(see Must Eat).*

Tides Folly Beach Hotel

$$$$ **132 rooms**
1 Center St., Folly Beach.
843-588-6464 or 866-599-6674.
www.tidesfollybeach.com.
For oceanfront digs on Folly Beach, you can't beat this full-service hotel. Chic, modern décor in the public spaces and rooms brings in the colors of the sea, while amenities include a mini-fridge, a flat-screen TV and free Wi-Fi. When

you're not enjoying the beach, you can take a dip in the heated pool or work out in the fitness room. Drop by **Blu** (**$$$**) for dining with a view or just to enjoy a cocktail on the beachfront patio.

Moderate

Fulton Lane Inn

$$$ **45 rooms**
202 King St. 843-720-2600 or
800-720-2688.
www.fultonlaneinn.com.
Since Fulton Lane Inn is hidden on a tiny lane off King Street, you'll be spared some of the noise from this busy commercial thoroughfare yet still have easy access to great King Street shopping right outside your door. King rooms have four-poster canopy beds, hardwood floors and in-room refrigerators; some even feature fireplaces and whirlpool tubs. The friendly staff is happy to help you make restaurant reservations and arrange tours and sightseeing.

Governor's House Inn

$$$ **11 rooms**
117 Broad St. 843-720-2070
or 800-720-9812.
www.governorshouse.com.
When Governor Edward Rutledge lived here in the late 1700s, this mansion, with its crystal chandeliers, nine fireplaces and double piazza (as porches are called in Charleston), entertained many local notables. Now you can stay here, equally close to The Battery and the historic district. Individually decorated rooms are outfitted with period furnishings, fresh flowers and hardwood floors; many boast private porches, fireplaces and whirlpool baths.

HOTELS

Amenities include free on-site parking, a continental breakfast, afternoon tea and evening sherry.

Hampton Inn Historic District
$$$ **171 rooms**
*345 Meeting St. 843-723-4000
or 800-426-7866.
www.hamptoninn.hilton.com.*
Adjacent to the Charleston Visitor Center, this former 19C railroad warehouse now welcomes guests in its incarnation as a Hampton Inn. Clean, comfortable rooms sport an antebellum décor, with mahogany furnishings and floral prints. Public areas boast pine floors and Oriental carpets. The hotel offers a pool, free local calls, and a complimentary breakfast bar.

The Inn at Middleton Place
$$$ **53 rooms**
*4290 Ashley River Rd.,
at Middleton Place Plantation.
843-556-0500. 800-543-4774.
www.middletonplace.org.*
You're sure to feel close to nature at this inn, located on the grounds of Middleton Place *(see Plantations).* Rooms are contemporary with floor-to-ceiling windows, plantation shutters, cypress

Two Meeting Street Inn

©Brigitta L. House/Michelin

paneling, handmade furnishings and braided rugs. With the price comes a full breakfast in the Lake House, evening wine and hors d'oeuvres and in-room snacks. Bicycles can be rented to explore the grounds. You'll also receive free passes to Middleton Place Gardens, the House Museum and Stableyards.

Two Meeting Street Inn
$$$–$$$$ **9 rooms**
*2 Meeting St. 843-723-7322
or 888-723-7322.
www.twomeetingstreet.com.*
At the tip of The Battery, this 19C home overlooks the water and is known for gracious Southern hospitality. The Queen Anne Victorian was built for newlyweds Waring and Martha Carrington in 1890. Inside, English oak woodwork, Tiffany stained-glass windows and crystal chandeliers bespeak the considerable means of the wealthy couple. Rooms have four-poster beds, most with lacy canopies. Ask the concierge to make dinner reservations and arrange for sightseeing tours or theater tickets.

The Inn at Middleton Place

© Middleton Place, Charleston, South Carolina

MUST STAY

Vendue Inn

$$$ **66 rooms**
19 Vendue Range.
843-577-7970 or 800 845-7900.
www.vendueinn.com.

Carved out of 18C warehouses, the Vendue Inn is a Charleston classic. No two rooms here are alike, but all are adorned with antiques and 18C reproductions. In some rooms, reproduction wallpaper and brick walls add historic charm, while Jacuzzi tubs provide modern luxury. All rooms offer robes, safes, air- and water-purification systems, and turn-down service.

Rates include breakfast, bedtime milk and cookies and use of bicycles. Try the continental cuisine at **The Library ($$$)** or light fare at the popular **Rooftop Bar** *(see Musts for Fun)*.

Vendue Inn
©Vendue Inn

The Westin Francis Marion

$$$ **234 rooms**
387 King St. 843-722-0600
or 877-756-2121
www.francismarionhotel.com.

Named for Revolutionary War hero Francis Marion (aka the "Swamp Fox"), this hotel premiered in 1924 at the corner of Calhoun and King streets, near shopping, restaurants, and the College of Charleston. Restored in 1996, the 12-story hotel encloses rooms with high ceilings and European style. Downstairs is the inviting **Spa Adagio** *(see Spas)*.

Inexpensive

Andrew Pinckney Inn

$$ **41 rooms**
40 Pinckney St. 843-937-8800
or 800-505-8983.
www.andrewpinckneyinn.com.

You can't go wrong for the price at this inn, well situated two blocks from Old City Market. The original 1840 structure was renovated in 2001, at which time the inn added six rooms and three townhouse suites in a new building across the street. Enjoy a complimentary breakfast on the rooftop terrace, while you scope out the sights.

The Ashley Inn

$$ **8 rooms**
201 Ashley Ave. 843-723-1848
or 800-581-6658. www.charleston-sc-inns.com.

Guests at this two-story gabled house, built in 1832, can take full advantage of the double piazzas cooled by ceiling fans. Rooms in the B&B are tastefully appointed with traditional furnishings, including canopy, four-poster or pencil-post beds; all have private bathrooms and cable TV. Start your day with complimentary orange croissant French toast or cream-cheese-and-chive scrambled eggs.

Indigo Inn

$$ **40 rooms**
1 Maiden Lane. 843-577-5900 or
800-845-7639. www.indigoinn.com.

Built in the mid-19C as a warehouse to store indigo, this building was converted into a bed-and-breakfast inn in 1979. Located a block away from the Old City Market, the inn

HOTELS

lodges guests in rooms outfitted with Colonial-style furnishings, some with four-poster beds. Most rooms overlook the brick courtyard, with its greenery and hot tub. In the morning, enjoy a complimenary breakfast.

The Grand Strand

Expensive

Island Vista
$$$$　　　**149 rooms**
6000 N. Ocean Blvd.,
Myrtle Beach. 888-733-7581.
www.islandvista.com.
This 12-story, all-suite hotel right on the beach is a perfect perch for family vacations. The more, the merrier, as accommodations range from spacious one- to four-bedroom suites. Family owned and operated, the Island Vista pampers guests with in-room spa services, two pools (one of them heated), a fitness center and fine dining. In addition, a full program of children's activities will keep the little ones occupied while you soak up some sun on the beach. For golfers, the hotel offers special Stay and Play packages.

Moderate

Anderson Ocean Club & Spa
$$$　　　**272 units**
2600 N. Ocean Blvd., Myrtle Beach.
843-213-5340 or 866-578-8494.
www.andersonoceanclub.com.
Choose among lovely studios and one-, two- and three-bedroom units at this new property, set on the ocean in the heart of Myrtle Beach. Tile floors, granite countertops and cherrywood cabinetry lend a luxurious feel. Amenities include a fitness room, indoor and outdoor pools, and Awakening Spa.

The Breakers Resort
$$$　　　**638 rooms**
Ocean Blvd. at N. 21st & 27th Ave.
N., Myrtle Beach. 843-444-4444 or
800-952-4507. www.breakers.com.
The Breakers has been a Myrtle Beach landmark for 70 years. Standard hotel rooms, most with balconies and many with microwaves and refrigerators, are done in light woods and tropical hues. The two towers added to the property feature one-, two- and three-room suites, and spacious condominiums. No matter which locale you choose, the kids will love the oceanfront water park.

Hampton Inn, Broadway at the Beach
$$$　　　**141 rooms**
1140 Celebrity Circle, Myrtle Beach.
843-916-0600 or 800-426-7866.
www.hamptoninnbroadway.com.
If you don't mind being off the beach, this Hampton Inn sits at the heart of the 350-acre entertainment complex Broadway at the Beach. Shops, restaurants, mini-golf, Ripley's Aquarium and many other amusements will be right outside your door. You'll also be treated to standard Hampton amenities such as free local calls and a complimentary breakfast bar.

Sea View Inn
$$$　　　**20 rooms**
414 Myrtle Ave., Pawleys Island.
843-237-4253.
www.seaviewinn.com.
(Room rate includes 3 meals a day.)
Open late Mar–late Nov.

Step outside the rambling, two-story Sea View Inn and you're literally standing on the sand—the inn's private beach. That, plus a friendly staff, three delicious meals a day, and the absence of phones and TVs, lure guests year after year. All rooms have air-conditioning and private half-baths. You'll find rocking chairs on the porch, books and board games in the living room and friendly conversation.

Inexpensive

Beach Colony Resort
$$ **240 units**
5308 N. Ocean Blvd., Myrtle Beach.
843-449-4010 or 800-222-2141.
www.beachcolony.com.
Beach Colony offers oceanfront suites, studio rooms with kitchenettes, and one-, two-, three- and four-bedroom condominiums. Swim in the indoor or outdoor pools, soak in the whirlpools, sip a drink at the oceanfront lounge or play racquetball in the resort's court. A lazy river tubing ride and a video arcade entertain the kids.

Ocean Creek Resort
$$ **299 rooms**
10600 N. Kings Hwy., North Myrtle Beach. 843-272-7724 or 800-621-2192. www.oceancreek.com.
This full-service resort offers accommodations from lodge efficiencies to three-bedroom oceanfront units.
Amenities include a restaurant, a sand volleyball court, a putting green, a separate pool for children, and a tram to ferry guests to and from the beach. Units in the North Tower are inviddivually owned, and all units are tastefully decorated.

Beaufort and Hilton Head

Luxury

Inn at Palmetto Bluff
$$$$$ **50 cottages**
476 Mt. Pelia Rd., Bluffton, SC.
843-706-6500 or 866-706-6565.
www.palmettobluffresort.com.
With its high-end amenities, this inn, overlooking the May River on 20,000 acres, caters to sybarites. The smallest rooms here are 1,140-square-foot cottages, with heart-pine floors, fireplaces, steam showers, and screened-in porches. That's not to mention wet bars, plasma TVs, Sub-Zero refrigerators, and DVD/CD players. Village homes, which come with two, three or four bedrooms, are perfect for families.
Avail yourself of the fine Lowcountry cuisine in the **River House ($$$$)**, the serene spa *(see Spas)* and the 18-hole Jack Nicklaus-designed golf course.

Expensive

Disney's Hilton Head Island Resort
$$$$-$$$$$ **123 units**
22 Harbourside Lane,
Hilton Head Island.
843-341-4100 or 407-939-7540.
www.disneybeachresorts.com.
Designed to look like a rustic hunting lodge, this resort has a laid-back feel. It's not on the beach, but it does own a private beach house reached via the hotel's shuttle. Choose from studios, or one-, two- and three-bedroom villas, the latter equipped with full kitchens. As you'd expect from Disney, there are activities for all

members of the family, from the Tot Lot playground to biking, kayaking and fishing for adults and teens.

Moderate

The Beaufort Inn

$$$ **25 rooms**

809 Port Republic St., Beaufort, SC. 843-379-4667 or 888-522-0250. www.beaufortinn.com.

Hospitality shines in this 1897 mansion in historic downtown Beaufort, which has entertained the likes of Julia Roberts and former CNN news anchor Paula Zahn. Each guest room is so uniquely decorated, you could stay in a different one every night and never get bored. Styles range from rich, dark Victorian to cotton-candy pastels with hand-painted furniture. Some rooms have wet bars; some have fireplaces; all teem with Southern charm. A full Southern-style breakfast and afternoon refreshments are part of the package.

Inn at Harbour Town

$$$-$$$$ **60 rooms**

7 Lighthouse Lane, Hilton Head Island. 843-363-8100 or 866-561-8802. www.seapines.com.

Casual elegance impresses you as you enter this sophisticated property, located near the Harbour Town Yacht Basin at Sea Pines Plantation. Rooms are custom designed with marble baths, soaking tubs and cotton Frette linens. Harbour Town Golf Links and the Sea Pines Racquet Club are just outside your door, and a short walk will bring you to the shops and restaurants of Harbour Town itself. The inn's accommodating

staff of English butlers are available to cater to your every need, from sending faxes to pressing clothes.

Main Street Inn & Spa

$$$ **33 rooms**

2200 Main St., Hilton Head Island. 843-681-3001 or 800-471-3001. www.mainstreetinn.com.

Luxury comes at a reasonable price at this Hilton Head inn. Modeled after a European boutique hotel, the Main Street Inn wraps guests in cushy comfort with brocade fabrics, hand-crafted armoires, and Frette robes. Luxury double rooms boast spacious baths, upscale linens and ceiling fans; some queen rooms have fireplaces; and roomy courtyard kings overlook a gurgling fountain. You may even be tempted to forego that golf game in favor of languishing by the pool, surrounded by fragrant gardenias. Rates include turn-down service, afternoon tea and a full American breakfast served in the sunny dining room.

Rhett House Inn

$$$ **19 rooms**

1009 Craven St., Beaufort. 843-524-9030 or 888-480-9530. www.rhetthouseinn.com.

The inviting double veranda of this inn beckons guests to gracious lodgings. Rooms are decked out individually in fabrics ranging from feminine pink florals to black-and-white toile; many have four-poster beds. Meet your fellow inn-mates during afternoon tea or evening wine and hors d'oeuvres. French toast, pancakes or eggs and grits are likely to greet you at the breakfast table. Rhett House makes a great base for exploring the area,

©Wayne H. Heath/Michelin

Rhett House Inn

but you might just as well simply settle back on the shady front porch and watch the world go by.

Inexpensive

South Beach Inn
$$ **17 rooms**
232 South Sea Pines Dr.,
Hilton Head Island.
843-671-6498 or 800-367-3909.
www.sbinn.com.
Located in Sea Pines Plantation, this inn tucks into a charming New England-style village complex of shops and restaurants. Accommodations, which are done in country décor and include one- and two-bedroom units, all have kitchenettes—making them ideal for families. The Atlantic Ocean lies just a few minutes' walk away, and guests here have access to Sea Pines amenities such as golf, tennis, watersports and bike trails. Breakfast is included in the room rate.

Savannah and The Golden Isles

Luxury

🏨 The Cloister
$$$$$ **175 rooms**
100 Salt Marsh Lane, Sea Island.
912-638-3611 or 855-714-9197.
www.seaisland.com.
Built by renowned Florida architect Addison Mizner, The Cloister has graced Georgia's Golden Isles since 1928. Today the original Cloister Hotel has been gracefully renovated. Guests who stay at the Lodge benefit from rooms overlooking the Plantation golf course; and at the Ocean Houses, visitors have access to five miles of private beach. While the kids are occupied with organized resort activities, you can escape to the Spa at Sea Island Resort *(see Spas)*, play a round of golf, or hit the tennis courts.

The Cloister, Black Banks Terrace

©William Torrillo/Sea Island

Greyfield Inn
$$$$$ **17 rooms**
On Cumberland Island. Ferry to the inn runs from Fernandina Beach, Florida. Two-night minimum stay.
904-261-6408 or 866-401-8581.
www.greyfieldinn.com.
Go to Greyfield when you really

HOTELS

Greyfield Inn

©Georgia Department of Economic Development

Go to Greyfield when you really need to get away; the inn, accessible by boat, is the only commercial establishment on the island. Built in 1900, Greyfield provides access to secluded Cumberland Island National Seashore. Rooms are decorated with Carnegie family heirlooms and antiques. Rates include three meals a day, use of bicycles and fishing and beach equipment. Note that there's no transportation on the island.

Moderate

Eliza Thompson House
$$$ 25 rooms
5 W. Jones St., Savannah.
912-236-3620 or 800-348-9378.
www.elizathompsonhouse.com.
Named for the society widow who built the stately house in 1847, this lovely B&B sits on a quiet street in Savannah's historic district. Each unique room is decked out in rich colors with four-poster or canopy beds and antique furnishings. You won't go hungry, as rates include a deluxe buffet breakfast in the courtyard, an evening wine and cheese reception, and desserts before bedtime. Another extra: guests receive a pass for the metered street parking.

The Gastonian
$$$ 17 rooms
220 E. Gaston St., Savannah.
912-232-2869 or 800-322-6603.
www.gastonian.com.
Attentive service defines Southern hospitality in the two adjoining Regency-style mansions that house this luxurious historic district inn. All guest quarters have working fireplaces and are elegantly appointed with Oriental rugs and antique four-poster, iron or carved wood beds. Many come with whirlpool tubs. For breakfast, you'll be hard-pressed to choose from a menu of entrées that include lemon cheese pancakes with strawberry glaze, a fruit and yogurt plate, and made-to-order omelets.

Jekyll Island Club Hotel
$$$-$$$$ 157 rooms
371 Riverview Dr., Jekyll Island, GA.
912-635-2600 or 855-535-9547.
www.jekyllclub.com.
Completed in 1888 as a hunting retreat for America's monied elite, this restored clubhouse, now a National Historic Landmark, retains its turn-of-the-century charm. The renovated historic Crane (1917) and Cherokee (1904) cottages offer additional luxurious rooms and suites. With 63 holes of golf (three

Jekyll Island Club Hotel

©Georgia Department of Economic Development

18-hole golf courses and one nine-hole course), 13 tennis courts, and a beach club nearby (free shuttle service is provided for guests), you may never want to leave the family-friendly complex. Save a night for dinner in the lavish Victorian **Grand Dining Room ($$$)**, which specializes in regional cuisine.

Inexpensive

Bed and Breakfast Inn
$$ **15 rooms**
117 W. Gordon St., Savannah.
912-238-0518 or 888-238-0518.
www.savannahbnb.com.

Bed and Breakfast Inn

©Georgia Department of Economic Development

The name may not be creative, but according to the owners, this historic district inn on Chatham Square was the first B&B in Savannah, opened in 1978. Air-conditioned rooms have private baths, TVs, and bonuses like irons and ironing boards and hair dryers. Rates include a full breakfast and afternoon tea, and the inn pays for your metered parking during your stay. A two-night minimum is required on weekends.

Green Palm Inn
$$ **4 rooms**
548 E. President St., Savannah.
912-447-8901 or 888-606-9510.
www.greenpalminn.com.
This 1897 Victorian houses guests in comfort in its four suites, each outfitted with British Colonial-style furnishings—a play on Savannah's British heritage. Each suite is individually decorated: the Royal Palm and the Sabal Palm suites boast two fireplaces each, including one in the bathroom. Bathrooms in both suites have clawfoot tubs. Guests at the Green Palm are treated to a full hot breakfast each morning and refreshments in the afternoon. The inn's staff will be glad to rmake restaurant reservations and arrange for city tours.

Mulberry Inn
$$-$$$ **145 rooms**
601 E. Bay St., Savannah.
912-238-1200 or 888-465-4329.
www.savannahhotel.com.
This pet-friendly historic hotel was built as a livery stable in 1860. Overlooking Washington Square in the historic district, the Mulberry Inn features traditional-style rooms nicely appointed in dark woods and hunt colors. If you're planning a longer stay, consider one of the units that have refrigerators and microwaves. Afternoon tea and pastries, a fitness room, and a pool and hot tub number among the amenities. You can grab a bite in the on-site cafe, and Sergeant Jasper's Tavern makes a cozy setting for an evening cocktail.

HOTELS

CHARLESTON, SAVANNAH AND THE SOUTH CAROLINA COAST

The following abbreviations may appear in this Index: NHS National Historic Site; **NM** National Monument; **NMem** National Memorial; **NP** National Park; **NHP** National Historical Park; **NRA** National Recreational Area; **NWR** National Wildlife Refuge; **SP** State Park; **SHP** State Historical Park; **SHS** State Historic Site.

INDEX

INDEX

INDEX